Picking Winners

Inspiring informative books for thoughtful readers wanting to make changes
and realise their potential.

Other titles in the series include:

Choosing a Better Life
An inspiring step-by-step guide to
building the future you want

Getting Your Next Job
A systematic approach to find the career
that is the best for you

Healing the Hurt Within
Understand and relieve the suffering
behind self-destructive behaviour

Please send for a free copy of the catalogue for full details
(see back cover for address).

Picking

Winners

A total hiring system for spotting exceptional performers and getting them on board

Steve Kneeland

PATHWAYS

First published in 1999 by
How To Books Ltd, 3 Newtec Place,
Magdalen Road, Oxford OX4 1RE, United Kingdom
Tel: 01865 798306 Fax: 01865 248780

British Library Cataloguing in Publication Data
A catalogue record for this book is available from
the British Library

Editing by David Venner / Cover image PhotoDisc
Cover design by Shireen Nathoo Design

Produced for How To Books by Deer Park Productions
Typeset by PDQ Typesetting, Stoke-on-Trent, Staffs.
Printed and bound in Great Britain

Note: The material contained in this book is set out in good
faith for general guidance and no liability can be accepted for
loss or expenses incurred as a result of relying in particular
circumstances on statements made in the book. The laws and
regulations are complex and liable to change, and readers
should check the current position with the relevant
authorities before making personal arrangements.

Pathways is an imprint of
How To Books

Contents

List of Illustrations

Preface

A good book – like a good movie – springs from the collaborative efforts of a number of people.

I would like to extend a heartfelt thank-you to the fine people of Johnson & Johnson Medical Products, in Canada, for whom a great deal of the material in this book was originally developed. Special thanks too must be directed to Susan McTavish, the forward-thinking head of the Human Resources area who has since moved on to exciting new challenges at the company's corporate offices in Texas.

To Pam, my wife – to Jessica and Jennifer, our two daughters, my grudging recognition of their forbearance and support. I am still not convinced that moving me and my computer out to the garden shed was absolutely necessary.

To Giles Lewis, the missionary force behind Pathways Books, and Nikki Read, the person whose job it is to turn otherwise good ideas into coherent and readable books, my sincere thanks for their professional assistance, encouragement, and patience.

Credit having been given where credit is due, you the reader may now judge the book by its merits and blame me for anything you don't like about it.

Steve Kneeland

CHAPTER 1

Average Isn't Good Enough

There is no shortage of books on how to interview job candidates. By and large, however, most books – there are one or two exceptions – take a fairly traditional approach to the subject. They may suggest some good questions to ask and tell you what to look for in the answers you get.

What we are doing in this book, however, is delving into the *process* that truly skilful interviewers use. As is true in most other skills, from playing the violin to kicking a football, what the truly accomplished practitioner does is largely intuitive and bears precious little resemblance to what one reads about in the standard beginner's manual.

In our experience, it boils down to two things:

◆ Having, inside one's head, a *behavioural model of what outstanding performance looks like*. A model based on what we have seen our top performers actually *do*.

◆ Interviewing the candidate in a way that cuts through the usual generalities and gets down to *the specifics of behaviour*. Who said what to whom and in what tone of voice?

That's the way a truly skilful interviewer goes about it. And that's the approach we're going to take in this book.

Every decision is crucial

The plain fact of the matter is that everyone we bring on board has to be capable of delivering outstanding individual performance. There is very little room – in today's corporation, and today's jobs, and today's marketplace – for average, run-of-the-mill performance.

Leaner corporate structures; the new emphasis on teamwork and communication and flexibility; the recognition that quality and customer service are fundamental requirements for business success rather than short-term fads; the need to deliver truly innovative solutions to increasingly complex customer problems; the ever-increasing demands being placed upon us by shareholders and parent companies; the volatile and brutally competitive nature of the markets we compete in...

This is a whole new world. There are few *easy* jobs left. Everyone has to be good. Everyone has to make a contribution to moving the business forward.

And that means that every hiring decision we make becomes a critical one. Critical to the growth and continued success of the business.

> Everyone we bring on board has to be capable of delivering outstanding individual performance.

New qualities are demanded

Hiring decisions aren't just more crucial than they used to be. They are also more *difficult*. And that's because the qualities we have to look for in people are in many cases quite different from what they were a scant five or so years ago.

Most managers and human resource (*HR*) professionals need little help when it comes to determining whether a person has the basic requirements needed to do a job. After even a brief initial interview, we usually come away with a fairly good sense of whether the candidate could 'do the job'.

Where most of us need help is in telling the difference between a good candidate and an outstanding one. In our experience, it boils down to the subtle things: critical thinking, intelligent risk-taking, initiative, strategic thinking skills, a sense of urgency, a sense of *mission*, the capacity for continuous learning and self-development, flexibility, spark, flair.

These aren't things we paid a lot of attention to in years gone by. And, in many cases, we're not terribly good at recognising them in people. More to the point, they are difficult to assess in the interview, even for a seasoned interviewer. But they get to the heart of what outstanding performance, in *today's* business climate and today's jobs, is all about.

Our goal in this book

This book is designed to achieve one very specific goal – and that is to hire people who will come on board, or move into the new job, and deliver outstanding performance.

The amount of time and money which a company invests in bringing a new person up to speed – and the amount of time that you as a *manager* have to invest – is considerable. And the difference between hiring someone who turns out to to be an *average* performer and hiring someone who turns out to be an *outstanding* performer, in terms of the actual results achieved, is substantial. So there's an awful lot at stake.

> Where most of us need help is in telling the difference between a good candidate and an outstanding one.

And yet – hiring people is something that a lot of us don't really enjoy and most of us haven't really been trained to do. We do the best we can, and we put a lot of time into interviewing candidates and making our final hiring decision, but it is usually not a nice, tidy process and we rarely come to the end of it feeling completely confident that we have hired someone who is going to be an outstanding performer.

Our goal in this book is to change that. To make the whole process a bit more systematic. A bit more logical. To give ourselves a clear strategy for the interview, a set of practical tools to use, and a coherent framework within which to assess what various candidates have to offer.

Summary

In this chapter we have introduced you to the importance of skilful interviewing in identifying and appointing winners.

We said there are two aspects to this process:

- ◆ Having, inside one's head, a *behavioural model* of what outstanding performance looks like.
- ◆ Interviewing the candidate in a way that gets down to *the specifics of behaviour.*

And that:

- ◆ Hiring decisions are more crucial and more difficult than they used to be.

◆ Interviewers must be able to differentiate between a good candidate and an *excellent* one.

◆ A more systematic process will help us pick our Winners.

CHAPTER 2

The Decision Would Be Easy

I magine being able to go out and actually *watch* a candidate perform his or her current job – for one whole day. You would see what time the person starts work in the morning, whether they're one of the first in or one of the last, what sort of shape they're in, how they go about organising their day, whether or not they organise their day at all. You'd hear them on the telephone, talking to people in other departments or to customers.

You'd see how they react when a problem crops up, whether they can shift gears quickly and leave this while they go and attend to that. You'd get a sense of whether they have their priorities in order – whether they recognise that, even though something might seem urgent and be crying out for attention, it might not really be as *important* as some of the other things on their agenda.

You would see what they're like face to face with the customer or with colleagues – how they handle a tough question or get around an objection, whether they listen carefully and pick up on what is being said. You would see how they react when something goes awry or a presentation falls flat or someone cuts them off before they've had a chance to cover the key things they wanted to cover.

You'd see whether they're cheerful and enthusiastic and full of spark, and you'd see whether they tend to droop a bit as the day wears on. You would see, too, what *results* they get. How those results compare to those of their colleagues. What help they got achieving those results.

The choice would be obvious

Here's the key thing. If you could do this for each of ten candidates for a given job – actually be a fly on the wall and watch each of them perform in their current job for one whole day – you'd have no trouble at all making a hiring decision.

You wouldn't even have to think about it. Your gut feel would tell you. You'd know *instinctively*. It would be an easy decision.

Or, if you could bring them on board

Or, if you could hire each of the ten candidates on a *trial* basis and watch them work on your team for a single week. Same thing. You'd know who to hire. Even if you couldn't analyse it logically, you'd know instinctively.

'Jim's not the kind of person we need around here. He wouldn't fit in. Betty's a good worker, but there's not enough spark there. No... Bill – Bill's the person I want to hire. Bill's exactly the sort of person I need on this team. Bill's my man. No question about it.'

Again, you wouldn't even have to think about it. Your gut feel would tell you. You'd know *instinctively*. It would be an easy choice.

Why the choice is obvious

Now why is that? If we could go back in time and watch each of ten candidates actually perform, or if we could hire them *all* on a trial basis and *then* decide who to hire, why is the decision so easy?

The answer is obvious. It would be an easy decision because we have *seen* the candidates perform. That is the key. That is what makes it easy.

The key is behaviour. The key is being able to *look* at how the candidate performs. The choice becomes obvious because we are looking at *real behaviour*. It's like taking a car out for a test run, or trying on a new suit, or sniffing the food in the cafeteria before deciding what to order for lunch. We are sampling the *real thing*.

When we do that – if we *could* do that – hiring people would be pretty easy.

> The key is behaviour. The choice becomes obvious because we are looking at *real behaviour*.

Rather than talking generalities, let's give ourselves an actual problem to solve. Let's imagine that we're interviewing a chap named John Harris, currently a sales representative with Acme Copiers Limited, and being looked at by ourselves as a candidate for a similar selling role within our own firm.

John's on the short list, having survived the initial cut and the first round of preliminary interviewing. So we'll be wanting to look at him very carefully and make some very pragmatic predictions about how he might perform if we decide to bring him on board.

So – what we're saying is that knowing whether or not we want to hire John Harris would be relatively easy if we could do one of two things – or both.

◆ Observe John's past performance. Actually go back in time and watch John perform his day-to-day duties at Acme Copiers.

◆ Observe his future performance. Leap ahead into the future and observe John in action as a sales representative in our own company.

Muddling through

Neither of these things, unfortunately, is possible. You can't be a fly on the wall and you can't normally hire people on a trial basis. That's what makes hiring people like John so difficult. You can't go back and observe how he's done things in the past, nor can you give him a 'try out' or a 'test run' in your own situation before making a final decision.

You can only *talk* to him – in an interview. And get an idea of how he has performed in the past. And, from this, develop a feel for how he might perform in the future.

It's a pretty tenuous business. Our only access to John's past performance is through his *description* of it. We can't *see* it. We can only see it through his eyes. His *description* of it is our only link.

Nor can we *see* his future performance. We can only *imagine* it in our mind. Our only handle on what he might do in the new position is through our own best *prediction* of future performance.

So we're dealing with second-hand data on the one hand,

and inferential data on the other. And there are some very real pitfalls on both sides of the ledger.

Objectivity or subjectivity?

One complication is that John, our candidate, is hardly an impartial or disinterested reporter. There's a job at stake, so we have to assume that he'll be putting his best foot forward. Even if that were not the case, there's still no guarantee that his report will be an objective and accurate one. It's hard, after all, to be objective when you're the main character in the story you're telling.

The difficulties on our side are just as great. If we could somehow be assured that John's description of his past performance was a complete and accurate and objective one, we'd still have a problem. Does the fact that he increased sales at Acme from £240,000 to just over £300,000 mean that he can come in and do the same thing for us? If it turns out that John's boss at Acme *knows* that he is out testing the market, and has done nothing to stop him, does that mean that John is no good?

You can see the problem we're faced with. The decision to hire someone is obviously a critical one with far-reaching implications for both the individual and the company – and yet the whole process seems to be hanging together by only a very thin and rather tenuous inferential thread.

> Trying to come up with a judgement about future performance is a struggle for the simple reason that there's so little to go on.

Still, the average once-in-a-while interviewer grits his or her teeth, pushes ahead bravely, and manages somehow to muddle through: trying to cover as much ground as possible, probing a bit here and there to make sure that all the usual bases have been adequately covered, and then struggling to come up with a reasonable judgement regarding the candidate's future performance in the new job.

It's tough, frustrating work. Trying to come up with a judgement about future performance is a struggle for the simple reason that there's so little to go on. We've gathered up a lot of 'facts' about the candidate's work history, education, achievements, and so on – but there's an awfully big gap between the scraping off of these surface facts and the subsequent prediction of future performance.

A better way

In this book, we're going to look at a new and improved way of interviewing. An *easier* way. We can't go back and be a fly on the wall. We can't jump *ahead* into the future and, in effect, watch people on the job for which they are being looked at as a candidate.

But we can come pretty close.

We're going to resort to the *next best alternative* – and that is to conduct the interview in such a way that we get down to the specifics of what a person actually did or said and how they went about it – that lets us come as close as is humanly possible to actually 'seeing' that person in action. We're going to take a *behavioural* approach to the interview.

Taking a *behavioural* approach to the interview means digging for the behavioural specifics of what happened in a situation. If our candidate, John, says that he was able to convince a customer to introduce a new product on a trial basis, taking a *behavioural* approach to the interview involves zeroing in on that incident and finding out what exactly happened, how the proposal was introduced, how the customer reacted initially, how that was actually *said* or *expressed*, how John responded, what happened next...

> Taking a *behavioural* approach to the interview means digging for the behavioural specifics of what happened in a situation.

In short, it means digging for behaviour. Who said what to whom and in what tone of voice. And then what happened after that.

By way of illustrating this, let's listen in on an interview that's already under way. The interviewer, Susan Miller, is asking the candidate – still John Harris – about his previous selling experience with Acme Copiers.

Interview

SUSAN: You just mentioned that you were able to bring in a number of new accounts while you were selling for Acme even though you were only there for a few months. Do you think we could talk a little more about that?

JOHN: It wasn't really very complicated, to tell the truth. The company names were given to me by my supervisor, and I was simply the one to make the initial contact.

SUSAN: What sort of guidance were you given? Did you and your supervisor sit down together, for example, and decide how best to make the initial approach?

JOHN: Not really. That was something I had to work out for myself. And I just used what I thought was good common sense.

SUSAN: Tell me a bit more, if you could, about what strategies you used – and why you felt they were appropriate.

Susan's obviously doing a lot more here than just carrying on a conversation. She's digging. Probing. Trying to work her way past the candidate's general descriptions and ferret out what was actually done. By whom. And why.

She's digging, and she will continue to dig, on that same specific point, until she's satisfied that she's got the real facts of this particular situation out on the table.

John, for his part, isn't being defensive. He's just doing what most people tend to do when they're in an interview – and that's sum things up in pretty general, global terms. Which is understandable. There's an awful lot that one could say about oneself and one's career, and only a limited time in which to say it. There's an almost universal tendency on both sides to want to cover a lot of ground in the interview. To be concerned lest some portion of the candidate's background isn't adequately covered. And the end result is an interview that skims over the surface, gathering general descriptions from the candidate but not really delving beyond them. Let's refer to this as the *horizontal* approach to interviewing..

What top interviewers do is take a *vertical* approach. One that digs down to the level of actual behaviour. Actual quotations. He said this and then I said that.

> Top interviewers take a vertical approach. One that digs down to the level of actual behaviour.

They don't talk in generalities. If the candidate says that one of his or her main achievements during the past year was landing the ABC account, the top interviewer doesn't let it go at that. He or she digs for the behavioural specifics.

'How is it that you targeted this specific account in your prospecting? What was the nature of your initial approach to them? Why did you do it that way? What reaction did you get? When you went in to see them, what did you do to prepare yourself? Why was that? How exactly did the meeting go? Were there specific concerns raised? If so, how did you counter them? Whose idea was it to bring the Director of Finance into the second meeting?'

And so on. *Who? What? When? Why? How?* Like a pesky newspaper reporter, the successful interviewer digs for the specifics of what happened. Landing the ABC account, he or she knows, means little in and of itself. What counts is *how* it was done. It is the candidate's behaviour that tells us what sort of performance we can expect if we bring the person on board. It is this performance, not the landing of the ABC account, that we are hiring.

We'll talk more about this in a later chapter, and we'll be introducing three very powerful interviewing tools which we'll use to put this behavioural strategy into practice. For now, however, the key point is this: *everything boils down to behaviour.*

◆ The closer we come to assessing behaviour in the hiring process, the more solid will be the foundation of the decision we make, the *easier* will be the decision, and the more *confident* we will feel about the decision we make.

◆ The further we stray from assessing behaviour in the interview, the more tenuous will be the foundation for our decision, the harder it will be to make that decision, and the less confident we will feel about it after it has been made.

> The key point is this: everything boils down to behaviour.

Summary

In this chapter we considered how we bring a candidate's qualities and performance into the interview situation.

- ◆ Ideally we want to see how the candidate *behaves* in different and demanding work situations.

- ◆ We need to somehow simulate the candidate's past performance.

- ◆ Then we can imagine the candidate's future performance.

- ◆ We looked at the difference between *objectivity* and *subjectivity*. The difficulty of identifying and dealing with real facts, second-hand data and inferential information.

- ◆ Remember that information from the candidate is not impartial.

- ◆ Trying to cover as much ground as possible, probing a bit here and there, covering all the usual bases before struggling to a decision *is not* the way to hire Winners.

- ◆ A behavioural approach to interviewing means zeroing in on an area and digging again and again until you have uncovered all there is to know about those claims or facts.

- ◆ Don't let the candidate talk in generalities.

CHAPTER 3

Personality Patterns

L et's say you had a good friend. Someone you have known for quite a few years now. And let's imagine that you were asked to predict how that friend of yours might do in the role of Press Liaison Officer for this year's local charity drive.

Your answer might well be something like this:

'Jane will work very hard, and she'll certainly show an awful lot of enthusiasm. And she'll relate very well to other people. But she's not really a very organised sort of person, and someone will have to keep an eye on how she handles the paperwork and schedules her time.'

And you'll say it *confidently*. You'll be comfortable with your prediction, and you won't have had to struggle to come up with it. And, more likely than not, your prediction will turn out to be an accurate and very perceptive one.

Now why does that seem so easy, whereas trying to decide whether or not to bring John Harris on board can be so difficult? There are a couple of reasons.

Predicting the future

The first reason is that you *know* Jane, whereas you've never met John Harris prior to your interview with him. You've actually *seen* Jane perform. You've watched her work, observed how she handled this problem or that, and seen what sort of results she was able to produce. So you're not just guessing. Nor are you having to go out on a limb on the sole basis of what Jane might have said about herself.

But it's more than this. It's not just that you know Jane, and you've had a chance to actually observe her behaviour. It's that you've seen *patterns* in that behaviour. Things she tends to do. Or not do. Certain ways she has of handling situations, relating to other people, or organising her activities. And you assume that those patterns will continue to show themselves in the future.

So you are predicting what she will do in the future on the basis of what she has done in the past. You are assuming that Jane will *continue* to demonstrate those habits which have been there in the past. There is, after all, no reason to assume otherwise – unless something very drastic has happened to alter Jane's whole approach to things.

And this assumption you're making is generally a safe one. There are certain things about people which *don't* change – at least not spontaneously or without reason – and Jane's tendency to be a bit disorganised is one of those things.

> A person's future behaviour is best predicted on the basis of past habits.

All this illustrates a very important point. One, in fact, that is the very foundation of our whole approach to selecting people. The point is this: a person's future behaviour is best predicted on the basis of those habits and patterns which have characterised his or her behaviour in the past. Let's expand upon that a bit...

Three basic assumptions

When you predicted how Jane would do in the role of Press Liaison Officer, what you were doing was operating on the basis of three very critical assumptions. Being conscious of these three assumptions, and putting them into practice, is the heart of what genuinely skilful interviewing is all about.

- There are patterns in people's behaviour.
- They can be seen in past performance.
- And they will be there in the future.

There are patterns in people's behaviour

If we look closely at the behaviour of a person over time, a number of patterns begin to emerge. There are common threads there, running through what the person does on a day-to-day basis and from one situation to another.

A person may avoid taking risks, for example, show sensitivity in dealing with people, be a bit careless with detail, tackle problems aggressively, or have difficulty standing back and seeing the forest through the trees.

The pattern won't *always* be there. A person who is aggressive and domineering by nature may not act that way when he or she is dealing with a visiting director in from head office. An individual who is highly meticulous and detail-minded by nature will hopefully be experienced and pragmatic enough to know when *not* to worry about crossing t's and dotting i's. The sensitive manager will know when to get tough with someone.

Still, a person's basic behavioural tendencies will never be too far from the surface. They will be there in the background, always pressing to get out.

> If we look closely at the behaviour of a person over time, a number of patterns begin to emerge.

They can be seen in past performance

If you look closely enough at a person's performance, you'll see the patterns showing through. At times, they'll be obvious – simply because they're shown so often and so consistently. But at other times we'll have to dig pretty deep.

We'll notice how one person has been consistently cautious and conservative in making career moves, all along the way, or how another has tended to flourish in turnaround-type situations, or how yet another person has always been good at doing detail work and staying within prescribed guidelines.

We'll see *connections*, too. The meticulous person who's good with detail may also tend to talk on and on about things, wandering away from the main point or the original question. The person who is aggressive in his or her dealings with people may tend to tackle straightforward *problems* aggressively, looking impatiently for a solution and perhaps tending to spin his or her wheels when faced with a subtle or complex problem for which there is no simple or direct solution.

The person who is good at organising things at work will probably tend to be well organised at home as well. You'll see it in how they organise a swimming party for the kids, how they organise an upcoming holiday.

And they will be there in the future

Here's another important point. These patterns of behaviour, usually learned early on in a person's life, don't usually change unless something very deliberate is done to change them. Even then, they seem to hang in there tenaciously.

Someone who's a perfectionist at the age of twenty-two will probably still be a perfectionist at the age of eighty-two. The young lad who bullied the other kids in the playground will probably end up being a boss who brow-beats his subordinates.

The patterns rarely change simply because they are so much a part of us, so much ingrained into our whole outlook and approach to things that we're not even *conscious* of them.

So – those patterns will still be there next week. And next month. And next year. They may show up in a somewhat different way, if it's a new job and a new environment, and they may not produce exactly the same results as they did in the old setting. But the basic patterns will still be there.

And this is the key to selecting people...looking for the behavioural patterns that have characterised them in the past, and acting on the assumption that these same patterns will continue to be there in the future. In doing this, we are relying on the fact that these basic patterns seldom change spontaneously – and that what a person has done in the past is, therefore, the best predictor of what he or she will do in the future.

> Those patterns will still be there next week. And next month. And next year.

The concept of personality

Let's do a couple of things at this stage, before going on to the next section.

First of all, let's bring in the word 'personality' to refer to the sum total of the patterns we might observe in a person's behaviour or performance.

And let's not be frightened off by the word 'personality'. It's simply a convenient way of acknowledging the fact that there are, indeed, patterns in a person's behaviour or performance. And these patterns, presumably, are caused by something.

If Cathy Winston is an active community leader, orders restaurant waiters around authoritatively, keeps a tight rein on her family's spending, barks at her dog, and tells us – in the interview – that yes, she enjoys being in a position of authority over other people... then it's pretty obvious that the word 'dominant', a personality term, would not be out of place.

All we are saying is that there is a common element in all of these bahaviours which, for the sake of convenience, we refer to as dominance. We conclude that there is something *internal* in Cathy's make-up which tends to express itself quite consistently in the form of dominant responses to individual situations.

It's not really all that important whether we think of the word 'dominant' as applying to the patterns themselves or to what's causing them. It amounts to basically the same thing.

In either case, we assume that there is an underlying source of continuity in a person's behaviour, a constant something-or-other that travels from one situation to another. And that it is this something-or-other that produces patterns in the surface behaviour – patterns that allow us to predict the future on the basis of what we know about the past.

So now we have a personality that underlies the individual's past performance and that will, presumably, show up again in the future.

The person's past performance and future performance, in other words, turn out to be two tips of the same iceberg. Personality is the link. It's the *bridge* between the past and the future. And it's the only bridge we have, so we have to use it.

> Personality is the only bridge we have, so we have to use it.

Our strategy for predicting the future

It should, by now, be clear what our basic strategy for predicting the future is going to be.

The strategy is simple, and it involves going through three distinct steps every time we interview. No matter who we're interviewing and no matter what kind of position is at stake.

Recreate past performance

We've already acknowledged that we can't go back and actually *observe* past performance. But the trick here is to come as close as possible. Using the candidate's description as our only guide, we have to re-create past behaviour as accurately and as realistically as we can – until we can almost see it unfolding before us in our own mind's eye.

In effect, we use the candidate's description as a doorway to the past. And go through it.

And that means a lot more than just asking questions. Or getting the candidate to talk. It means digging. And probing. Breaking through the barrier of the candidate's generalisations and assumptions and interpretations and distortions – and getting at the *facts*. The behavioural facts of what actually happened. Who said what to whom. And how it was said. And what happened next.

Look for 'personality' patterns

They're there. If you look hard enough for them. And if you've done a good enough job of getting the behavioural facts – the raw data, so to speak – out on the table.

A good interviewer is always operating on two levels. On the behavioural or *performance* level, he or she is digging away to unearth the facts of what really happened. On the *personality* level, the interviewer is constantly searching for patterns – looking for common threads, drawing up hypotheses, testing them out by further probing, modifying or rejecting those that don't hold water, building upon those that do.

And attaching words to them. We move from saying '*He did such-and-such*' – an observational fact – to saying '*He tends to do such-and-such*' – an inferential conclusion ... from saying this is what he *did* to saying this is what he's *like*. He works well under stress. He looks at things methodically. He manages people with a firm hand. He doesn't suffer fools gladly.

This is the inner world of interviewing. A rarefied space that many of us never get to operate in. But it's *here* that the really good interviewers spend most of their time. It is here that we stop just gathering information, and start doing something with it.

> We use the candidate's description as a doorway to the past. And go through it.

Visualise future performance

We've now come full circle. We've gone back through the candidate's past performance, then gone down from there into the realm of behavioural patterns and personality. Now we're coming up again. On the other side of the iceberg. We've bridged the gap as shown in Figure 1.

This final step involves projecting what we've learned about the person into the future. Not logically. *Visually.*

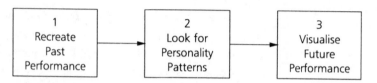

Fig. 1. Visualise future performance.

Imagine the person sitting in on the Tuesday morning staff meeting, or handling that sales call that you watched Keith Chalmers botch up yesterday afternoon, or standing in the booth beside you at next month's trade show in Madrid.

Create the future, in your mind's eye, just as vividly as you did the past.

You can only really do this well if you've done a good job of going through the other steps. The more systematically and the more consciously you've gone through the first two steps, the more vivid and the more useful will be the image that emerges from the third.

> This final step involves projecting what we've learned about the person into the future. Not logically. *Visually.*

Strategy versus technique

It is more important that you go away with this simple, three-step strategy firmly embedded in your mind than to send you away armed with a plethora of neat interviewing techniques. It's more important that you understand the *process* – that you see the common-sense *logic* involved.

You could probably put this book aside right now, in fact, and come away a better interviewer. Your mindset would have shifted a bit. Your approach to the interview, your *strategy,* would be a bit different.

Yes, there are techniques that we'll be looking at. And we'll keep them as practical and as helpful as possible. But you *could* stop here. If you wanted.

Indeed, if this is all we did – take a *behavioural* approach to our interviewing of candidates – we would add significantly to the effectiveness of our hiring. We would be better interviewers and we would do a better job of making decisions about people.

It would happen because we would come away from the interview with a much clearer image of how a given candidate is actually going to perform should we decide to bring him or her on board. We would have seen the person in action. We would know what we were getting.

The really top interviewers, as it turns out, don't stop here. They go one step further...

Summary

In this chapter we have looked at becoming familiar with patterns in people's behaviour and how we might use them for predicting future performance.

There are three basic assumptions

- ◆ There are patterns in people's behaviour.
- ◆ They can be seen in past performance.
- ◆ And they will be there in the future.

And we can say that:

- ◆ Used properly, they become a tool for predicting future performance because you've experienced the candidate working and achieving results in the past. You've seen patterns of behaviour.

♦ You're eliminating some of the guesswork from the interview process.

♦ These patterns of behaviour, usually learned early on in life, don't usually change as one gets older. If someone is organised now they will be for the foreseeable future.

♦ The candidate's past performance and future performance are two tips of the same iceberg. Personality is the link between the two.

♦ Don't be frightened off by the word 'personality'. In this context it is the term used to describe the sum total of a person's behavioural patterns.

♦ 'Personality' is the link between the past and the future so don't be afraid to use it.

We looked at this simple strategy

♦ Recreate past performance

♦ look for personality patterns and

♦ visualise future performance.

CHAPTER 4

Pinning Down What's Needed

What we have outlined thus far is a basic approach to the selection interview. A basic strategy that will get us around the gap that separates what we know about the past from what we'd like to know about the future.

What a person has done in the past is the best predictor of what he or she will do in the future. The underlying behavioural patterns which have shown themselves before will most likely continue to do so. This simple idea, as we have said, is one of the cornerstones of our approach to selecting people.

But it is not enough. It is not enough to simply predict a person's behaviour. To make a *hiring* decision, we also need to know whether that behaviour is what's needed for successful performance on the job.

> We need to know what behavioural patterns we are seeking for.

We need, in short, to know what behavioural patterns we are looking for. We need to know what specific patterns of behaviour will lead to success in the job – and which will be harmful or irrelevant.

What are we looking for?

This is the other half of the selection coin. Knowing what we are likely to get is not enough. We also need to know what we are looking for.

It's a crucial question that each manager has to ask him or herself. What *are* the key things which make for successful performance in this job? In this particular division or this particular region of the country? At this particular point in time? And under me as a manager?

In short, what are the specific things I should be looking for when I interview and then evaluate a candidate for the job?

Targeted interviewing

The second part of our strategy for the interview, then, involves going in with a clear image of what sort of behaviour we are looking for. It involves taking a *targeted* approach to the interview.

Targeted means that we dig for behavioural specifics in a selective fashion. Our goal isn't simply to 'watch' the candidate perform, it's to watch him or her perform in certain areas or in relation to certain situations. We need a model that gets to the essence of what we mean by outstanding performance – in *this* company, in *this* segment of the business, with *you* as the manager.

So the question becomes – *What do the top people in this job actually do?* What is it about their behaviour, about how they actually do things on a day-to-day basis, that accounts for their being our top performers?

> *Targeted* means that we dig for behavioural specifics in a selective fashion.

Knowledge and skills

Let's start with the *job description*. There's usually one available, and it's the logical place to start in our effort to pin down what's needed in the job.

If it's like most job descriptions, it will outline the key duties and responsibilities involved in the job as well as the reporting relationships, number of people supervised, and – perhaps – the goals that have to be achieved or the performance standards that must be satisfied.

There will usually be, too, a description of what the job *requires* in the way of knowledge, skills, and job-related traits or qualities. And it is in this section that we are most likely to find clues as to the sorts of qualities that we should be targeting in our interview.

Let's start with the most tangible and clear-cut of these items – the knowledge and skill factors.

Knowledge factors

Most jobs require a certain level of what might best be called *technical* knowledge or 'expertise'. It might be a knowledge of standard costing systems, or electronic circuitry, or market research. Or it might be a bit broader... marketing know-how, a good grasp of business fundamentals, a good basic understanding of how to manage people, insight into the reality of how you get things done in a big company like this.

When people trip up due to lack of *knowledge*, it is typically in these latter areas – the broad ones. They have an insufficient grasp of business principles. They don't understand how the system works. They have an inadequate insight into their customer's business. They don't really understand what people in other departments within their own company are doing.

Skill factors

Skills, like knowledge, aren't directly observable, but we *can* see them being used – or not being used. By examining each of the areas of responsibility in a job description, it is usually not too difficult a task to list what skills are going to be needed.

Planning skills, analytical skills, conceptual skills, presentation skills, the skills of persuasion and leadership... these generic skills are of increasing importance in most jobs. In some jobs, there will be additional skills – project management skills, systems analysis skills, mechanical skills – which are quite specific and technical in nature.

Again, when people trip up, it's not usually due to a lack of technical skills. More often than not, it's the broad and intangible skills that are the culprit.

Looking for outstanding performance

Our focus throughout this book is going to be on how to hire people who can come in and give us not just *acceptable* performance but *outstanding* performance. And we'll do that for the reasons we outlined in Chapter 1. These days, increasingly, acceptable or average performance *just isn't good enough*.

Knowledge and skill factors, by and large, are minimum standards. They get at what's required for *acceptable* performance. Their presence will in most cases not be a guarantee of outstanding performance, in other words, but their *absence* might well be an *obstacle* to outstanding performance.

So we'll use them primarily in the screening phase of the hiring process, as a means of sorting out the people we should interview versus those who'll be relegated to the back burner or rejected as unqualified.

> Knowledge and skill factors are minimum standards. They get at what's required for *acceptable* performance.

Focus on behaviour, past and future

We need something more. Something that gets at what *outstanding* performance in the job is all about. The job description tells us that the ideal candidate will be a good communicator and a good team player and will be able to work effectively with minimal direction and will be an ambitious person who wants to get ahead in life.

Now that's getting us closer to the mark. But just how helpful are these statements? They sound rather general. Again let's talk strategy.

We've already established that our approach to assessing what a candidate can do is going to be to focus on behaviour – past behaviour. We're going to look for how a person has actually behaved in the past and then project that behaviour into the future.

It makes sense, then, to retain the same behavioural focus when it comes to defining what it is we're looking for. What sort of *behaviour* are we looking for? That's going to be the question.

The job description as it stands probably doesn't tell us how the ideal incumbent should *behave*. The general prescriptions it contains – should be a good team player and have good communication skills and be able to function effectively with minimal supervision – are not quite explicit enough to be deemed behavioural.

We're going to need to do something a little bit out of the ordinary.

Looking at what people actually do

To describe behaviour we have to start by *looking* at behaviour. To define what sort of behavioural patterns are needed in a job, the most logical thing to do is look at the behaviour of people already *in* that job.

So, at this juncture, we ask two very important questions:

◆ What are the specific behaviours that I see in my people that seem to account for them producing good results? What specific behaviours do I see that I wish *everyone* would display?

◆ What specific behaviours do I see in my people that seem to produce *poorer* results? What are the things that people do which appear to *impede* successful performance?

> To define what sort of behavioural patterns are needed in a job look at the behaviour of people already *in* that job.

Once we have pinned down the bits and pieces of behaviour that seem to spell the difference between good and bad – or outstanding and average – performance, we begin sorting them into meaningful patterns and finding a name for each pattern.

Let's imagine, for example, that we're managing a team of internal IT consultants serving the needs of system users throughout our organisation. Meetings with internal customers, both to identify needs and to review progress, are critical. In thinking about what makes our top people successful, we might notice that they all seem to do the following:

◆ They take a half-hour at the outset of the day to think about what lies ahead and sort out the priorities.

◆ They spend at least a half-hour thinking ahead to prepare for any important meeting.

◆ They go into a meeting with a clear agenda that has been written down on paper.

◆ They have thought through their answers to the key questions they might be expected to deal with.

◆ They know what they want to come away with – what *outcomes* they want to achieve.

Clearly, there's a *pattern* here. My top people seem to do a good job of planning. So I'll call it that – *Planning*. Planning is one of the things that I have to look for when I bring a new person on board. And I'll give high marks to candidates who do the same sort of planning that I see my top performers doing.

So – that's how we know what's needed. That's how we know what specific patterns of behaviour to look for when we interview a candidate. We identify the specific *behaviours* and behavioural *patterns* that produce successful results. We look at what our top performers actually *do*.

> Identify the specific *behaviours* that produce successful results. Look at what our top performers actually *do*.

Don't be lazy

The job description says that 'good communication skills' are needed to do this job effectively. That's fine. It's a useful pointer. Someone has gone to the trouble of thinking about the job and putting together a list of the performance characteristics that are going to be important.

My advice is this – take it with a grain of salt. Treat the list as a useful starting point. Go out there and see for yourself what specific behaviours are producing outstanding results and what specific behaviours are *impeding top-level* performance.

Good communication skills? You don't have to look any further than Rita Malone. Here are just a few of the things that you might have noticed during the past week:

- She's good at making small talk and getting people to relax, but she doesn't overdo it.
- She makes a point by giving you the overview first, then the details, and then she goes back and reiterates the overview.
- She actually made Jacques Beaudoin *smile* the other day. That's got to be a first.
- She can be gung ho and bubbly when talking to the sales people and yet be very businesslike, even downright *analytical,* when dealing with our technical people.

And here's the important thing. These behaviours that we see in Rita are a large part of what accounts for her being an outstanding performer. She didn't just make Jacques smile – though that's an amazing accomplishment in itself – she got him to smile and go along with the very same proposal that he had rejected out of hand just a month ago.

So, if Rita's job is the one that we're going to be hiring for, then, yes, communication skills are a must. And – looking at what Rita does – we know good communication skills when we see them.

Look for yourself. That's the message. Treat the job description as a taking-off point. Go out there and check for yourself.

> Treat the job description as a taking-off point. Go out there and check for yourself.

Let's not oversimplify things

We're emphasising, here, the importance of knowing what we are after. The idea is that we analyse what makes our successful people successful and then look for those characteristics in the people we hire. It seems like a logical thing to do. And it *is* logical.

Still, there's a potential problem in this approach if it is carried too far or applied too literally. So let's take a moment to talk about it. Here are the pitfalls:

- ◆ The pattern is rarely a clear-cut one.
- ◆ People can compensate for shortcomings.
- ◆ A good quality can be carried too far.
- ◆ What's needed can change.
- ◆ Technical specifications can be over-emphasised.

> There's a potential problem in this approach if it is carried too far or applied too literally.

The pattern is rarely a clear-cut one

If we look at virtually any job, we will find certain skills or attributes that simply have to be there. An order entry clerk has to have basic keyboard skills. A sales representative has to have a certain level of persuasive skill. An inventory control manager has to know how to control inventory. These have-to-be-there ingredients usually define a *minimal* level of acceptability. With them, a person has a chance. Without them, he or she should not be hired.

Once we go beyond the obvious, however, the pattern is less clear-cut – and it is never really possible to pin down exactly what any given job requires for successful performance. In the case of most jobs, indeed, the job performers tend to be rather unique in how they achieve their results. They may be alike in certain respects, but not to the point where one can say that there is a single definitive *model* that defines successful performance.

People can compensate for shortcomings

Even if we knew for sure that a certain skill or attribute was needed for success in a particular job, we would still have to be careful. People have a way of making up in one area what they may be lacking in another, and thus can sometimes confound our assumptions about what is needed.

A person may be quite average when it comes to being a 'self-starter' and displaying initiative, for example, but may achieve outstanding results through good planning and faultless organisation so long as he or she is working with clearly defined goals and well-established guidelines.

Or, a person may be a little bit arrogant and may tend to rub certain people the wrong way, and yet *still* be an outstanding performer in the sense of producing superb bottom-line results.

A good quality can be carried too far

This is another and more subtle danger. A desirable characteristic – be it assertiveness, concern for detail, persistence, or even intelligence – can begin to have not-so-desirable consequences if taken too far.

In searching for the person with assertiveness, we may inadvertently hire the one who irritates people with his or her aggressiveness and inability to listen. Or, by emphasising the need for *stick-with-it-ness*, we may find ourselves hiring an employee who ends up beating his or her head against a brick

wall or who has trouble responding flexibly and
opportunistically to unforeseen circumstances.

Every strength can become a liability if carried to extremes
or used inflexibly without regard for the demands of the
situation at hand.

So we have to be very careful here. Yes...we want the
candidate to be a self-starter. That makes sense. But how *much*
of a self-starter?

What's needed can change

A common error is to hire in accordance with the needs of *last
year's* company – rather than next year's. We hire the person
needed to solve yesterday's problems rather than the one
needed to take advantage of tomorrow's opportunities.

We're operating in an increasingly fluid and competitive
business environment. The person we hire *this* year will have to
be better than most of the ones we might have hired three
years ago. And the ingredients needed to produce outstanding
performance in the job will not be the same as the ingredients
we were looking for back then. Jobs are more complex. The
skills needed to do them have changed. Managers are *managing*
people differently. The total business environment in which we
have to do our managing has become much more volatile,
much more complex than it used to be.

> Hire the person needed for next year's company.

What's needed can also *vary.* A laid-back style might
produce good results in one region of the country, for example,
whilst a more aggressive approach might be just what's needed
in another. There may be *departmental* differences. The people
over in Judy's area get lots of clear directions, because that's
the way Judy likes to manage. The people in Lucy's area,
although they do basically the same type of work, have to fend
for themselves. That's just the way Lucy tends to manage.

Technical specifications can be over-emphasised

A common hiring error is that of placing too much emphasis
on technical qualifications or specific experience requirements.

The fact of the matter is that people usually succeed in a job, or fail, for reasons which have more to do with operating style and interpersonal skills and attitude and character than with technical skills or knowledge per se – and there is no reason why they should not be hired on the same basis.

Technical qualifications and specific experience requirements should be used as criteria in the broad screening phases of the selection process, not as a reason for hiring or not hiring.

How will this person actually perform?

There's another, more subtle danger involved in drawing up lists of specific traits and qualities and credentials that we feel a candidate's got to have in order to be a good candidate.

The danger is this: *It affects the way we interview people.*

It leads us to make the mistake of worrying too much about the sort of person we are *looking for* – rather than what sort of person we've got sitting in front of us.

Too many interviewers spend too much time looking to see how a given candidate matches the 'specs' – rather than simply sitting back and trying to get a feel for how each individual candidate would actually perform the job if given the opportunity.

If you *do* give people a chance – if you project each one into the job and actually 'watch' them perform, so to speak – you'll find that there are all sorts of interesting ways of getting a job done.

Choosing people should be, in most cases, a lot like wandering into a cafeteria and deciding what to eat. You know you're hungry. But you don't really know what it is you wish to eat. And you won't know until you've had a chance to browse around a bit, take a sniff or a nibble here and there, and let your taste buds and olfactory nerve-endings respond to what's on the menu.

That's what you do, after all, when you're choosing a car. Or deciding what house to buy. Or even buying a new suit, for that matter. You take the car out for a spin, and get a feel for it. You don't just buy it out of a magazine. You wander through the house and imagine what it would be like to live in it. You don't just let your agent choose it for you. You try the suit on for size and look in the mirror to see what it does for you. You don't just buy it right off the rack.

And there's no reason why we shouldn't be doing the same thing when we're picking people. Giving them a chance to tell their story. Projecting them ahead and 'watching' them perform. Getting a feel for how they – as individuals – would handle themselves in the new job.

Interviewing people should be an exciting job. One that's lively, and stimulating, and full of discovery and challenge. But it can't be if all you're doing is sifting through bodies until you find one that matches the 'specs'.

> Don't worry – during the interview – about *evaluating* their predicted performance. Focus all of your attention on *predicting* it.

So the strategy is this – When you interview a candidate, focus all your energies and attention on discovering how that specific person will function, how they will do the job...

Don't worry – during the interview – about *evaluating* their predicted performance. Focus all of your attention on *predicting* it.

Assume they've been hired

So – assume they've got the job. Assume they've been hired. They're going to be starting on Monday.

Focus all of your attention on *how* they are actually going to perform.

That's going to be our strategy. Write it down somewhere. Memorise it. It's an important strategic decision.

Assume they've been hired. They're going to be starting on Monday. Focus all of your attention on *how* they are actually going to perform.

But let's address an obvious question. If we're going to assume that the person has been hired, why do we have to worry about pinning down what's needed to *do* the job? Unless we're going to *evaluate* the candidate, why bother drawing up a list of performance criteria.

Because it operates in the background. That's the answer. It sharpens our instincts. It gives the little black box inside us something to chew on.

It's like buying a house. It's helpful to sit down and make a list, on paper, of the various things that you want or don't want in a house. It's helpful to be as specific as possible – so that you can almost close your eyes and *picture* the house and walk around inside it.

But then you can throw out the list. It has done its job. Your subconscious has stored the criteria away somewhere, and your instincts will draw upon them judiciously when the time comes to react to an *actual* house. You won't just be using 'gut feel'. You'll be using *educated* gut feel.

That's the way the mind works.

Summary

In this chapter we have looked at whether a candidate's behaviour, and therefore their predicted performance, is suitable to the requirements *of this job*.

♦ Start by examining the job description. This will define the key skills, knowledge, qualities and responsibilities required of the successful candidate.

♦ We asked ourselves *what* do the top people in this job actually do? *How* do they do it? What skills do they utilise when being successful?

♦ Decide beforehand upon the behavioural patterns you are actually looking for in the candidate that will help to bring success *for this job*.

♦ Remember that successful behaviour and successful skills are inextricably linked in a real winner.

♦ Adopt the same *behavioural* focus when it comes to deciding *what* you're looking for.

♦ This will help you take a *targeted* approach to the interview where you keep digging for the answers you want.

There are potential problems, though, if you oversimplify this approach.

Remember that:

The behavioural pattern is rarely a clear-cut one.

◆ Candidates can compensate for shortcomings.

◆ A good personal quality can be carried too far.

◆ What's needed for success in this job now can change in the future.

◆ Technical specifications can be over-emphasised.

◆ Don't spend too much time on a rigid system of seeing how a candidate fits the job specification. Instead project them into the job. Visualise how their behaviour would equip them to *do the job*. Get a feel for the candidate.

There is a core
set of behaviours
that set
successful people
apart from the
average.

CHAPTER 5

The Winner's Profile

Y ou can see the quandary we're faced with. Our approach
to the interview, we have said, is going to be both
behavioural and *targeted*.

The *behavioural* part is a second-best alternative. The ideal
would be to go back in time and actually *watch* our candidates
perform in a previous job, or watch them at work in *our*
environment. We can't do that, but we'll come as close as we
can by digging for behavioural specifics during the interview.

What about the second part of our strategy? *Targeted.*
Targeted at what? We have said that, when we watch a person
perform, we instinctively compare what we see to a *model* that
we have in our head of how a really *top* performer performs.
So the answer is – *targeted* at the things which we see in our
outstanding performers.

But we don't know what your people *do*.

They might be internal IT consultants. Or customer service
representatives. Or regional sales managers. We don't know.
And that's because this book has to serve the needs of a wide
array of management-level readers.

The Winner's Profile

Fortunately, there's a way to deal with the situation. Indeed, it's
an approach we would probably take anyway, even if we *didn't*
have the quandary to deal with.

We're going to make an assumption.

> Certain people are successful no matter what challenge
> they take on.

Winners possess certain qualities regardless of whether they
are internal IT consultants, customer service representatives,
regional sales managers, housemakers, or politicians. There is a

core set of behaviours – of habits, of habitual ways of doing things and looking at things – that set successful people, in *all* walks of life, apart from the average.

◆ Goal Orientation
◆ Organisation
◆ Initiative
◆ Intelligence
◆ Relationship-Building
◆ Communication Skills
◆ Leadership
◆ Enthusiasm
◆ Drive
◆ Resilience
◆ Self-Development
◆ Stayability.

These are the twelve ingredients of what we'll call *The Winner's Profile*.

There are other things, of course. Things that are unique to this or that specific position. The *Winner* who is an internal IT consultant will have the uncanny ability to make a computer sit up and do tricks. The *Winner* who is a regional sales manager will display a toughness and *gravitas* which spells 'leader' the minute he or she walks into the room.

But our twelve ingredients are the core. Certain people are going to be successful no matter what challenge they take on, and it is because they possess a high level of these 12 core success qualities which we have listed here and which are summarised briefly in Figure 2.

And that simplifies our task as interviewers. It allows us to focus on one simple, undeniable fact.

We need to hire successful people.

Not just people with a successful attitude or the *potential* to be successful ... but people who are, in actual fact, *successful.* Successful in school, in previous jobs they have had, in their hobbies, in their marriage, as parents...

We can give people lots of resources to work with ... good products, superb training, a good territory, a world-class corporation, a superb brand name ... but we can't teach them to be successful. They have to bring that in with them.

1. **Goal Orientation**: Has the candidate set specific and realistic personal goals?

2. **Organisation**: Has the candidate pursued those goals in a systematic and well-orchestrated manner?

3. **Initiative**: Has the candidate demonstrated the ability to act independently and *deal* with situations?

4. **Intelligence**: Has the candidate demonstrated the ability to solve problems and make intelligent decisions?

5. **Relationship-Building**: Has the candidate built effective relationships which stand up over time?

6. **Communication Skills**: Is the candidate able to get *through* to people and sell ideas?

7. **Leadership**: Has the candidate demonstrated the ability to lead and motivate other people?

8. **Enthusiasm**: Do we see enthusiasm – especially in regard to the *goals* the candidate is pursuing?

9. **Drive**: Do we see the will to succeed – in the form of focus, determination, and tenacity?

10. **Resilience**: Is the candidate able to take problems and setbacks in their stride and learn from them?

11. **Self-Development**: Does the candidate work systematically to develop personal *effectiveness*?

12. **Stayability**: Do we see the promise of a good fit between the candidate and the organisation?

Fig. 2. The Winner's Profile.

> The twelve factors form the *target* portion of our *behavioural* and *targeted* interview strategy.

It is this built-in capacity to be successful that is the common thread running through the twelve factors on *The Winner's Profile*. They are what go together to form the target portion of our *behavioural* and *targeted* interview strategy.

Our challenge in the interview

Let's reiterate.

The Winner's Profile identifies 12 specific characteristics of successful people. The key point is that certain people are going to be successful no matter what challenge they take on, and that is simply because they have developed or acquired certain characteristics, or habits, which are the key to success in any field.

If they can bring those characteristics into *our* company or organisation, provided they have the fundamental *knowledge* and *skills* that are needed in the specific job under consideration, they are going to be successful. Our challenge in the interview is to find out whether those characteristics are there. They provide the *target* of the interview.

And this provides us with the essential structure for the interview. Everything else – what questions to ask, what 'techniques' to use, when to do this and when to do that – is just a means to an end.

The goal of the interview is to answer the twelve questions on The Winner's Profile accurately and without having to ask them directly of the candidate.

Our goal is to answer the questions *on the basis of evidence* – which means without having to resort to asking the candidate directly. That's our acid test. If we can't answer one or more of the questions accurately and on the basis of indirect evidence, then we call the person back in and do another interview.

So the rules are:

◆ You have to answer all twelve questions following the interview.

◆ You have to answer 'Yes' or 'No' to each of the questions. *In-between* or can't decide or *unsure* means 'No'.

◆ You have to do so without asking the question directly of the candidate. You have to judge for yourself, on the basis of evidence you gather about the candidate's behaviour.

> The goal of the interview is to answer the twelve questions on *The Winner's Profile* accurately and without having to ask them directly of the candidate.

Let's talk a bit about the twelve factors on the profile.

Factor 1: The starting point

Successful achievement – and that is the bottom line that we are after – begins with a goal.

1. Goal Orientation

The first quality is *Goal Orientation*. We need to know that the candidate has developed the habit of setting specific goals and working toward their achievement – something which is characteristic of *all* successful people. There is a *focus* to their behaviour, a sense of direction, a sense of *mission*.

Factors 2–4: Day-to-day execution

The next three qualities have to do with *how* the person pursues his or her goals.

2. Organisation

The second quality is *Organisation*. We need to know that the candidate pursues their goals in an intelligent, disciplined and *effective* manner – planning ahead, focusing on the things that count, not getting side-tracked by things that have little chance of paying off or by details that are not critical to the central task at hand. We need to know that the candidate works *effectively*.

3. Initiative

The third quality is *Initiative*. We need to know that the candidate is the sort of person who takes the bull by the horns and gets things done, without having to be prodded or given the go-ahead. Who takes *action*, who doesn't sit around waiting for things to happen. If there is one thing that *Winners* all have in common, it's *Initiative*.

4. Intelligence

The fourth quality is *Intelligence*. We need to know that the candidate is bright enough to think on their feet. See what is happening in a situation or where a discussion is leading, master the challenge of learning that every new employee faces, and generally meet the intellectual requirements of the job to be done and preferably the job *after* that as well. As the business world gets more complex, the demand for analysis and strategic thinking is pushed further and further down the corporate ladder, and the room for error diminishes, then the importance of the *Intelligence* factor – as part of *The Winner's Profile* is heightened with every year that passes.

Factors 5–7: Dealing with people

In pursuing one's goals, a person – everyone, these days – has to work with and through people:

5. Relationship-building

The fifth quality that we are going to be looking for is *Relationship-building*. We need to know that the candidate is the sort of person who builds good relationships with people and is a good team player who can establish rapport quickly and readily in initial encounters, can bridge the gap that so often separates departments and functions, and will be an asset – simply in terms of being the sort of person who is good to have around – to you and your team as a whole.

6. Communication Skills

Everyone, these days, has to be a communicator. And *Winners* are especially good at it. The acid test is that they get through to people. They convey information effectively. They are able to communicate ideas and concepts as well. They *speak* well, and they recognise the all-important fact that communication is something that happens in the minds and hearts of the audience – not the words of the speaker.

7. Leadership

The seventh factor is *Leadership*. We need to know that the candidate is confident and assertive enough to move a discussion along and make sure that certain key points are covered. That they can impose deadlines or standards on other people without necessarily having the authority to do so; to effectively represent your team's interests on a cross-departmental committee or task force and stand up strongly in defence of any idea or proposal. This list goes on and on. There are few if any jobs these days in which the *Leadership* factor does not set the truly successful performer – the *Winner* – apart from their peers.

Factors 8–10: The inner person

Three *inner* qualities play an absolutely vital role in the successful achievement of one's goals.

8. Enthusiasm

The eighth factor is *Enthusiasm*. We need to know that the candidate is a positive, up-beat, enthusiastic kind of person who enjoys their work, who gets keenly involved in things, and whose manner *communicates* their enthusiasm to other people. It's not enough to *be* enthusiastic. It has to be a vibrant, visible quality that other people can *see* and – what is even more important – be affected by. *Winners* don't keep their enthusiasm quietly to themselves. They spread it around.

9. Drive

The ninth factor is *Drive*. We need to know that the candidate is the sort of person who aims high, who doesn't settle for average, who – once a goal has been set and committed to – doesn't rest until that goal has been achieved. We don't want to hire average people. We need to hire *outstanding* people. And outstanding people – *Winners* – achieve outstanding results in large part because they are *determined* to achieve outstanding results.

10. Resilience

The tenth factor is *Resilience*. We need to know that the candidate is someone who can rebound quickly following a setback, who doesn't dwell on things and who has a thick skin. That's simply because truly successful performance in any field is never easy. Results don't come quickly and they don't come without requiring that we deal with a lot of obstacles, hurdles, problems and frustrations along the way. *Winners* are confident people, by and large, and their self-confidence is not so fragile or tenuous as to be diminished by the occasional setback.

Factors 11–12: Additional characteristics

Finally, two factors which do not have to do with goal achievement *per se* – but are critical:

11. Self-development

The eleventh factor is *Self-development*. We need to know that the candidate is someone who practises continuous learning. Good people are *always* learning, always working on their own effectiveness, always searching for ways to put their talents to optimal use and maximise the results they achieve.

12. Stayability

The twelfth factor is something we're going to call *Stayability*. A *Winner* who joins us in April and leaves at the end of August isn't going to do much winning – at least not for *us*. We need to know that the candidate will stay with the organisation long enough to repay the considerable investment that both you and the company will be making in their success. There's no room for error here. We can't afford to hire good people and then have them leave after only a year or a year and a half on the job.

These, then, are the twelve factors that make up *The Winner's Profile*. They are the *target* for the interview – the qualities that we are going to be looking for. Taken as a whole, they do not guarantee that a person will be an outstanding performer if he or she is brought on board. But it is difficult to imagine someone being a truly outstanding performer *without* them.

Summary

In this chapter we have analysed a proven winner's profile and agreed there is a core set of behaviours that set successful people above the average. We then recommended the *targeting* interview approach as a method of identifying a candidate who possesses these behaviours.

There are twelve elements to the Winner's Profile

- ◆ Goal Orientation
- ◆ Organisation
- ◆ Initiative
- ◆ Intelligence
- ◆ Relationship-building
- ◆ Communication Skills
- ◆ Leadership
- ◆ Enthusiasm
- ◆ Drive
- ◆ Resilience
- ◆ Self-development
- ◆ Stayability.

Other things that are specific to a particular job are important too. The IT consultant who can make a computer perform tricks. The linguist who communicates with overseas clients.

We are looking for a candidate who will bring these characteristics into our company.

CHAPTER 6

Judging the Candidate on Paper

There is usually a point in most hiring situations where we have to judge candidates on *paper*. This is most obviously the case when we have either placed an ad in the paper or are having candidates sent to us by an agency. In either case, our first contact with the candidate is through a CV – and that CV is sometimes one of *many* that we have to go through before deciding which candidates to interview.

The CV gives us our first opportunity to look at the candidate, even if only on paper, and it is an opportunity that should not be taken lightly. The CV is more than just a formality. It is an integral part of the selection process, and it has a number of important purposes to serve.

> The CV is an integral part of the selection process, and it has a number of important purposes to serve.

For one thing, it is a concise and rapid way of getting some basic information about the candidate into your hands. Name, address, telephone number, education, job-related training, professional or industry involvements, and hobbies.

Most useful, of course, is the summary of the person's work experience with dates, company names, job titles, and details of what was involved in each position. The CV may also indicate salary, special achievements, and reasons for leaving each job.

If you had to use time during the interview to obtain all these vital pieces of information, there would be precious little time left over to get down to the crucial task of exploring how the candidate actually *performs*.

So the CV is an integral part of the total selection process. It is the first step in a series of progressively demanding hurdles over which the individual candidate must pass in order to land the job. And it is the CV which allows you, the manager doing the hiring, to boil a large group of candidates down to a manageable number before actually investing valuable time in interviews.

Don't just *read* the CV. Digest it. Take notes. Force yourself to generate as many hypotheses about the candidate as possible. Decide, most importantly, what areas of information may need to be specifically probed or explored further in the subsequent interview should you decide to proceed to that step.

Remember, though, that it is too early to pass judgement on most candidates, so that what we are drawing up here are hypotheses, not conclusions. Keep that in mind as we go through the various parts of the CV and look at the information which they contain.

> Don't just *read* the CV. Digest it. Take notes.

Work Experience

Let's start with the obvious – the outline of the candidate's *Work Experience*. Does the candidate have the sort of experience needed to do the job for which he or she is being considered? That's the first and most obvious question that has to be raised.

To answer it, you'll have to look beyond the mere job titles reported on the CV. Look at what specific things the person was *responsible* for in each position. Look at what segment of the company they worked in, who they reported to, what specific products they were dealing with, what projects they were working on, what things – other than their formal 'job' – they were involved in.

Look for *results*. What, specifically, has the person achieved? How significant are those achievements in the light of what you know about the product or project they were dealing with or the company they were working for?

The candidate who does not present their results – whose CV tells you what he or she was *responsible* for but not what specific outcomes were accomplished – should be suspect. There is no excuse for an *outstanding* candidate not telling you what they have accomplished. A run-of-the-mill applicant might get away with it. But not a *Winner*.

In assessing a candidate's work experience, the rule of thumb is this. Look for people who have already done the kind of job you want them to do for you, and have done it *successfully*.

In a *sales* hiring situation, for example, give them one point for having any sales experience at all. Give them another point for having worked in our industry, and another for having handled a competitive or related product line. Give them a point for having handled a line that matches your own in terms of breadth and complexity even if it is in a totally different field. Give them a point for having called on the same type of customer that your people are calling on.

And so on. That's the process we have to go through as we look at the specifics of where a person's career has taken them.

> Look for people who have already done the kind of job you want them to do for you, and have done it *successfully*.

Educational Background

Then look at *education*. Look, first, at how *much* education. Is there enough there to suggest that the person has at least an average level of intelligence if not better than average? By and large, the key here is the presence of something beyond the secondary school level.

Then look at what *sort* of education. The ideal is probably a blend – some 'hard stuff' such as chemistry and biology and genetics to suggest that the candidate has an affinity for technical subject matter...and then some 'soft' stuff such as history and literature to suggest that the candidate is a well-rounded person with broad interests.

Keep your eyes open for the possibility of a candidate having *too much* education, or having advanced education that has not been used in any obvious way. We have reason to raise an eyebrow if the candidate has spent years taking college or university courses that are totally unrelated to the career that they have since pursued.

Look carefully, too, at the specific subjects which the candidate has taken. Are the courses uniformly difficult ones, or are there a lot of 'soft' courses thrown in? Do the courses tend to be in the hard, tangible disciplines or in the more abstract, theoretical ones?

The answers to these questions can tell us a lot about the candidate's motivational attributes, or about his or her affinity for tangible problem-solving as opposed to abstract theoreticising.

Career progress

It is always important to look at what progress a candidate has made during his or her career. The person who has moved along rapidly might well expect to continue such movement – and this can be both a positive sign of motivation and drive and ability, or a warning of potential frustration.

> Look for signs that what you are seeing is the summary of a *progressive* career.

Make sure that it is a career *progress* you are seeing – not just movement. As you glance through the CV as a whole, look for signs that what you are seeing is the summary of a *progressive* career. It should hang together. The educational part should support the subsequent work history, the work history should do justice to the education, and the career as a whole should give evidence of forward *movement* as the candidate expanded their scope and took on increasingly challenging assignments.

If a person has had several jobs, on the other hand, but has not made significant progress in terms of the scope of his or her responsibilities, it raises a number of questions. The person may lack drive and ambition. They might be avoiding the taking on of broader responsibilities and the shouldering of higher levels of pressure.

It can be worrisome, too, to note that a person has spent more than five or so years in the *same* job. Companies, as a rule, don't usually let a really good performer linger too long in one job or at one organisational level.

But don't be too quick to judge. And, when you do judge, do so in the form of a *hypothesis* that will need to be tested out in the interview. Don't draw firm conclusions at this stage unless you're on very, very solid footing.

Career Stability

Look, too, for *Career Stability*. This is the other side of the coin. Beware of the candidate who has changed jobs frequently, particularly if the changes have not been accompanied by visible career advancement.

It may be that the candidate works in two-year cycles – just long enough to master a job before becoming bored with it and anxious to move on to something new. Or we may be looking at a marginal employee – a decent worker, perhaps, but one of the first to be laid off when business slows down or the organisation decides to trim staff.

Again, don't judge too quickly. There are many good people out there whose careers have taken on a rather 'choppy' look through no fault of their own. In this era of mergers and acquisitions and buy-outs and shut-downs, it's not uncommon for a good person to move through two or three different companies in quick succession.

Too much stability, of course, may indicate a lack of ambition or a tendency to be complacent or a reluctance to take risks. What we need to see is a mature, judicious balance between too much hopping around at the one extreme and too much standing still at the other.

Portable Assets

What tangible skills, experiences, training, insights, or product knowledge does the candidate bring with them into the job? These are what we'll call the *Portable Assets*.

Generally speaking, the more portable assets there are, the less adjustment will be needed and the more immediate will be

> The more portable assets there are, the less adjustment will be needed and the more immediate will be the candidate's contribution.

the candidate's contribution. Look carefully at what is there, and at how much of it can be transferred to the job for which the candidate is being considered.

In a sales candidate, look especially for familiarity with your distribution channels. The exact product might not be critical but the more the person knows about *who* you sell to and *how* you sell to them, the better.

If the job is in manufacturing, operations, materials management or distribution, look at how closely the individual's background overlaps with the ins and outs of your own environment. Especially in terms of such things as software, equipment, costing methods, and so on.

If the position is that of customer service representative, look at the range and complexity of the products that the candidate has been accustomed to and the specific types of problems or enquiries that they've had to handle. Look, too, at how much supervision they are used to, and how much customer contact.

Communication Skills

Communication Skills – that's something else we should be looking for. The CV is our first glimpse of the candidate as a *communicator*. If we were one of this person's customers or colleagues, and this is how they communicate, would we be impressed?

Is it an *organised CV*, for example? There should be some logic in the way the information is laid out. It should be an intelligent presentation which makes it easy for the reader to digest the basic facts at a glance. And those facts should be clear and specific. Give high marks to the candidate who, in listing their achievements, avoids vague generalities and gives you specific facts and verifiable numbers.

We have to look, to, at the *appearance* of the CV. Sloppy handwriting, scratched-out errors, uneven margins, mistakes in grammar or spelling, or indeed, a too-obvious effort to impress using flowery language, excessively ornate or expensive paper.

None of these things are knock-out factors. But they don't make a good impression. They wouldn't impress our customers or colleagues, certainly.

This is the important thing: what you see is representative of the individual. We have to assume that this person will approach customers and colleagues in exactly the same manner they have approached us. We have to put ourselves in their shoes, and assume that what we are seeing here is a representative sample of how the candidate operates. Hire someone whose initial presentation is sloppy or ostentatious – writing it off in your mind as due to lack of job-hunting experience – and you will most likely live to regret it.

Indications of attitude

Many applicants give information which is inadvertently

revealing. When describing their reasons for leaving a particular job, for example, the candidate might write that

'I left because of a disagreement over policy' or *'I was never given a fair chance'* or *'I could not see eye-to-eye with my supervisor.'*

Statements like these indicate an inability to adapt to the corporate environment, or a tendency to put the blame on other people. Their mere *presence* on the CV may suggest a certain degree of naivety.

Attitude-wise, what the CV should convey is a judicious blend of courtesy, professionalism, assertiveness, self-confidence, humility, and organisation of thinking. Anything that rubs you the wrong way should be cause for concern, unless the reaction stems from a purely personal bias. Trust your instincts here.

Indications of initiative

The candidate who has worked evenings in order to get through school may be more self-reliant and resourceful than one whose education was financed by others. Clues like this should not be ignored.

Again, it is too early to be drawing definite conclusions. What we are trying to do is generate reasonable *hypotheses* based on the information we have available – hypotheses to be either validated or rejected during the interviewing to come.

The Covering Letter

Look carefully at the *Covering Letter*. The letter which came with the CV is perhaps even more critical than the CV itself, because it is – or ought to be – addressed to our specific situation and our specific needs.

If the candidate is responding to an ad, and did *not* include a *Covering Letter*, you should be very tempted to scratch them off your list right away. Sending in a CV without taking time to compose a *Covering Letter* is like throwing a brochure into an envelope and sending it out to a prospective customer. It's not only ineffective, it also signals a basic lack of courtesy and is quite likely to get the recipient's back up.

When you read the candidate's *Covering Letter*, think of it as a *sales* letter, with you as the prospective customer and the candidate as the product. And then ask yourself whether what you're reading is an *effective* sales letter.

If the letter tells you that this person is *exactly* what you are looking for then chalk up one strike against the candidate. Without having talked to us in person, the candidate doesn't know enough about the job to make that sort of claim. If they tried that sort of thing on a real customer, it wouldn't get them very far. Not with *our* customers, at least.

If the letter is full of the candidate's own *self-evaluations* –

'I am a creative thinker with a flair for developing innovative business solutions' –

be sceptical. Good candidates usually present their achievements and let those achievements speak for themselves. They don't *tell* you that they are creative. They are confident enough to let that fact shine through in a straightforward outline of what they have achieved.

In general, the *best* covering letter will represent a mature down-to-earth effort to sell the idea of your inviting the candidate in for an interview. The top candidates will write a covering letter that says, in effect:

'I read your ad with great interest. It would be presumptuous to claim, on the basis of just the ad, that I am the ideal candidate – but I wouldn't be writing to you today unless I felt that the basis for a good "match" seems to be there.'

> Good candidates usually present their achievements and let those achievements speak for themselves.

The candidate's Follow-up

There's another important piece of information that we have access to at this early stage – and that's what a candidate does *after* sending their CV for your attention. The question here is whether or not the person *Follows-up* – and how they do it.

> What you are seeing here is how the candidate does things, and it's safe to assume that what you see is representative of what customers and colleagues would see if this person were to be hired.

Does a candidate who takes time to make a follow-up call deserve extra marks? Yes, as long as it's done professionally and maturely. Someone who makes a nuisance of him or herself – and you will know the difference – deserves to *lose* a few marks. Again, trust your instincts. What you are seeing here is how the candidate does things, and it's safe to assume that what you see is representative of what customers and colleagues would see if this person were to be hired.

Sorting the candidates out

The CV is the *first step* in the selection process. Like all other steps in the process, its purpose is to help us screen some candidates out and allow others to move on to the next step.

Screening a candidate out at this stage means that you are deciding – on the basis of the CV, and without even *talking* to the candidate – not to proceed any further. That's an important decision, and it should be made on the basis of something fairly obvious and tangible. The person has skipped around from one job to another during the past ten years, for example, or has no experience at all in our industry, with our type of customer or with our whole distribution set-up.

> The decision should be made on the basis of something obvious and tangible.

How comfortable you feel making such judgements at this stage will depend largely on the *Selection Ratio* you have to work with. A high ratio means that there are a lot of candidates to choose from – it is a 'buyer's market' with you being the buyer – and you have to take steps to whittle the total group of candidates down to a manageable number.

You can do it in one of two ways:

Sort the CVs into two piles

One for those who are obviously unsuited for one specific reason or another. And one for those who warrant a closer look. Applicants in the first category can be informed of the negative decision at this stage – using a routine form letter – and applicants in the second category can be invited in for interviews.

This is the strategy to use when there is a relatively small number of candidates applying for the position.

Sort them into three piles

This is the strategy to use when there is a relatively *large* number of candidates. Keep one pile for those, again, who are obviously unqualified or unsuited.

Create a second pile for those who really stimulate your interest, the ones you are genuinely anxious to interview. And keep a third pile for all the others.

In doing this, we have to seek a judicious balance between two conflicting factors. The first is the need to minimise interviewing time. The second is the need to do *enough* interviewing to ensure that the person we end up hiring is among the best available, if not *the best*.

Each manager will have their own decision-making 'style' here. Some are more cautious than others. Some shy away from making intuitive or broad-stroke decisions and prefer to digest all the available data before arriving at a final choice.

Some are prepared to hire the first top-notch candidate they see, while others aren't comfortable until they have looked carefully at *all* the top candidates and carried out a systematic comparison.

> Judging people on paper is difficult, and, if we are going to err at all, it is probably best to err on the side of letting *too many* candidates get through this first critical screening test.

Find your own balance here. It will depend on both the prevailing Selection Ratio and your own decision-making style. But beware, as a general rule, of putting either *too much* or *too little* emphasis on the CV as a screening tool. Judging people on paper is difficult, and, if we are going to err at all, it is probably best to err on the side of letting *too many* candidates get through this first critical screening test.

Summary

In this chapter we have looked at the importance of the CV in the interview process.

- ◆ It is a concise and rapid way of acquiring personal details about the candidate.

♦ It provides us with a summary of the candidate's work experience.

♦ Take notes from the CV. Digest it properly. Use it to help build the picture of past behaviour.

♦ Use it as part of the preliminary screening process of the interview. The first step in identifying our successful candidate.

♦ Look for *results* in the CV.

♦ Look for what's *missing* from the CV.

Look for certain core elements

♦ Work Experience.

♦ Educational Background.

♦ Career Progress.

♦ Career Stability.

♦ Portable Assets.

♦ Communication Skills.

♦ Indications of Attitude.

♦ Indications of Initiative.

♦ Look, too, for a Covering Letter.

♦ Make sure the application is unique to our company and not one that was computer re-generated.

♦ What Follow-up activity did the candidate employ?

♦ Use it as part of the *targeting* interview process.

CHAPTER 7

A Plan for the Interview

A t this point, then, we have a general strategy for the interview. We can't actually go back in time and *watch* a candidate perform, nor can we observe their behaviour by hiring them on a trial basis before making our decision. But we're going to come as close as we can – by taking a *behavioural* approach to the interview. That's our strategy.

And we know what sorts of behaviour we're going to be looking for. We're going to be looking for the very same patterns of behaviour that we see in our top performers.

Interview preparation

We have organised this book around the idea of there being two interviews. The first is where we screen the candidates. The second is where we probe more deeply.

Now... let's get ready for the interview. Let's assume that you have a young lady named Susan coming in to see you at two o'clock this afternoon. What should you be doing to get ready?

Preparation is an important part of any interview. The experienced interviewer knows that what lies ahead is something more than just a 'conversation'. A lot of information has to be gathered in a limited period of time, and the interview will be the basis for some very critical decisions. It calls for the same degree of forethought and preparation that one would apply to an important sales presentation or management meeting.

There are three important things you have to do to get ready.

◆ Make sure your purpose is clear.
◆ Review the available information.
◆ Plan out what you wish to cover.

Make sure your purpose is clear

This should be obvious, but is well worth noting here just for emphasis. Many a manager wanders aimlessly from one topic to another during the interview simply because the objectives which he or she is trying to reach have been only vaguely and generally established. The result is wastage of valuable time – and usually a confused or irritated candidate as well.

Take time, therefore, to make sure that the purpose of the interview is clear. For *this* interview – the first – our purpose is quite clear. It's to see whether the candidate has the basic personal qualities needed to be an outstanding performer, and to decide on that basis whether to advance to a second interview.

> For the first interview our purpose is quite clear. It's to see whether the candidate has the basic personal qualities needed to be an outstanding performer.

But in other interviews, at other stages of the selection process, the purpose will be different. You might be probing more deeply into some troublesome points that have emerged in your previous discussion with the candidate. Your goal might be to narrow things down to a short list. If you have only a single decent candidate, your purpose might be to decide whether to take a risk with that person or go back to the drawing board.

What exactly will you be trying to accomplish in the interview? It's a question we have to ask ourselves each and every time around.

Review the available information

Long before Susan comes into your office, you should be familiar with her educational background, work history, training, hobbies, and so on. These and other facts will all be available on the CV.

Or, if you are further ahead in the selection process, you will want to review the results of the testing procedure, look over the comments made in references, or read through the notes of other people who have interviewed the candidate.

By studying all the information available, you will be in a

better position to plan out the interview so that as little time as possible is devoted to things which have already been covered or ascertained.

Plan out what you wish to cover

This is something that every experienced interviewer does – and it pays handsome dividends. A good plan ensures an even coverage of all the areas that are important, and allows the discussion to flow smoothly from one area to another with a minimum of hesitation or awkwardness.

Before the interview begins, you should sketch out the main topics you wish to cover, determine more or less how much time should be devoted to each, and make a note of any specific questions or points which need to be included along the way. Make the plan as detailed as possible, even while recognising that there will be a certain degree of flexibility in how it is executed.

Do we need to plan?

Before we go too much further, let's ask a simple question – do you *need* a plan? Would it not be better to just meet the candidate and allow the discussion to unfold in a spontaneous, unrehearsed fashion? Is there not a danger, if we try to plan out the interview ahead of time, of our meeting with the candidate being stilted and regimented?

Let's answer that. And let's acknowledge that some interviewers *don't* sit down and plan things out ahead of time.

> For most of us, interviewing is so much easier when you take time to develop at least a rough idea of what you wish to talk about.

By and large, though, the ones who don't go into the interview with a plan are those who have been interviewing people long enough to become very *good* at it. They don't need to plan out each and every interview because they have settled on a standard strategy which has become a very intuitive part of how they conduct every interview. The plan is there, but it's there in the background. It's becoming part of their natural approach to interviewing.

For most of us, interviewing is so much easier when we take time to develop at least a rough idea of what we wish to talk about. What areas, in what order, with a view to collecting what sort of information? Having such a plan does two important things for us.

◆ It keeps us in control of things.
◆ It helps us cover what has to be covered.

It keeps us in control of things

A novice interviewer tends to worry a lot about the one thing that he or she really shouldn't have to worry over ... what to talk about. In the planned interview, because there is a definite sequence of topics to be discussed, the interviewer is never in the position of having to wonder what to talk about next.

There's less rambling, fewer false starts and fewer unproductive side-journeys. Once a particular topic area has been thoroughly explored, the direction is clear – and a simple 'Let's move on a bit, now, and talk about ...' is all that is required to bridge the gap.

And that, in turn, helps us relax and concentrate on what is going on. The interview shouldn't be hard work. We should not always be wondering what to talk about or how to move on to the next subject.

It helps us cover what has to be covered

Our interview is going to have to cover a lot of ground. We can't afford to spend an hour talking about the person's education and work history, for example, and then have to rush through a cursory discussion of his or her thoughts about the future.

A *plan* for the interview ensures that the candidate's background is reviewed in a complete, comprehensive manner. When all the relevant topic areas are explored systematically, there is less danger of us giving too much emphasis to one or two of them at the expense of others – and less danger of our impressions being based on a limited sampling of the candidate's experience.

The Plan

So – we're going to take a *planned* approach to the interview. We're going to go in with a fairly clear idea of what things we're going to talk about and the order in which we're going to talk about them.

There's no single best way to do this. But here's a plan of attack that seems to work well with most people.

We start with a brief warm-up period, a bit of small talk to get the candidate into the office, seated, and feeling reasonably relaxed.

Then we talk about the basic purpose of the interview, what we will be trying to accomplish, and how we will do it. We make sure the basic ground rules are clear.

We then begin our discussion of the candidate's background, and probably the best place to start is with a look at their formal education.

Then we move into a chronological review of the person's work history, starting with the first job they had upon leaving school and working through to their current or most recent position.

Now we talk about their career goals and aspirations – where they see their career going from here, where they would like to be five or so years down the road.

Then we talk specifically about why the job in *our* particular company or organisation is attractive to them, how it fits into their career plans and how it will help them get where they want to go.

Finally, we put work-related issues aside altogether and spend the last portion of the interview talking about family and social life. Chat about their hobbies, the *personal* side of things.

> It's not *essential* that you do it in this order. But it *is* essential that you *have* an order.

That's our *Plan* for the interview. Warm-up. Ground rules. Education. Work history. Career goals and aspirations. This job and this company and then personal life and hobbies. Those are the areas that we are going to cover.

It's not *essential* that you do it in this order. But it *is* essential that you *have* an order – for the reasons we outlined earlier. There's an awful lot to talk about in the interview, an awful lot of ground to be covered, and having a *plan* is the only way to make sure it gets done.

A tight squeeze

Two observations. First, this is a *lot* to squeeze into an hour-and-a-half interview.

The second observation is this. Because there is so much ground to cover, we are compelled to move things along smartly and not dwell too long on any one subject. This is the *opposite* of what we said we were going to do and that's to take a *behavioural* approach to the interview. Our goal, as you recall, is to come as close as is humanly possible to going back in time and actually 'watching' the candidate at work. That means talking about *behaviour* – who said what to whom, and in what tone of voice, and then what happened next. And that takes *time.*

So we have to proceed very carefully. This is why planning, and learning how to *stick* to that plan once the interview is underway, is so important.

The first of two

Remember we have organised this book around the idea of there being two interviews. The first interview is where we do our initial screening of candidates, and some candidates will fall out of the race at this stage. The second interview is where we take a more in-depth look at the select group of people who have survived the initial cut.

In practice, that is generally how it works. We rarely if ever hire a person on the basis of only a single interview and there is almost always some degree of screening needed to get the number of finalists down to a manageable size.

In some hiring situations, there might be two or even three 'second' interviews. Another manager might get involved once you have decided that a person is worth moving ahead with, for example, or the candidate might spend some time with someone in Human Resources or with one of the senior executives.

But – from the standpoint of the interviewing that you do in order to narrow things down to a single candidate – it seems realistic to think in terms of two interviews. An initial screening interview with what might be a dozen or more candidates and then a more in-depth assessment of the few who make it through the initial screen and find their way onto the short list.

Our goal in the first interview

Let's make sure that our goal, as we head into our initial interview with the candidate, is clear. We alluded to it briefly on an earlier page. Let's go back and make sure that it is absolutely crystal clear in our mind before going on to the next chapter.

Our overriding goal – the *big* goal – is to build a successful organisation. Our more *specific* goal is to hire people who will be outstanding performers and who will be that way long enough to pay back the considerable investment that we have made in them.

Every time we bring someone on board, we have to do so with the confidence that this person is going to achieve outstanding results and that the results which they achieve will more than repay the huge investment that we – both you the manager, and the company – will be making in terms of time and money.

> Our goal is simply to decide whether or not the candidate deserves to move on to the next stage and be given a second interview.

Our goal in the first interview is *not* to make a final hiring decision. It is important that we be clear about that. Our goal is not to come away knowing that the candidate is the best available person for the job or that he or she would be an outstanding sales performer. Our goal is simply to decide whether or not the candidate deserves to move on to the next stage and be given a second interview.

Summary

In this chapter we have prepared for the interview and reminded ourselves again that we will adopt a behavioural approach with the intention of establishing patterns of past behaviour.

We identified three important elements in preparing for the interview.

 ◆ Make sure your purpose is clear.

 ◆ Review the available information.

 ◆ Plan out what you wish to cover.

We agreed a plan was desirable because:

 ◆ It keeps us in control of things.

 ◆ It helps us cover what has to be covered.

 ◆ There are dangers in letting the interview unfold in a spontaneous, unrehearsed, fashion.

 ◆ Remember that time is always at a premium and you have a lot to squeeze into the average hour-and-a-half interview.

 ◆ Because you have so much ground to cover you need to move the process along smartly. This must be handled carefully because you've taken a behavioural approach to the interview. You need to balance your time budget against the length of answers you seek from the candidate.

 ◆ Remember that our goal in the first interview is merely to decide whether the candidate moves on to the next step in the process.

CHAPTER 8

Getting Started

I n this chapter, we're going to get the ball rolling. We're going to get our first interview with the candidate underway.

We've said, in putting together our *Plan* for the interview, that there are two preliminary tasks that have to be taken care of right at the outset, before we move into a discussion of the candidate's background.

First, we need a brief warm-up period, a bit of small talk to get the candidate into the office, seated, and feeling reasonably relaxed.

Second, we need to talk about the purpose of the interview – what we will be trying to accomplish, and how we will do it. We need to make sure that the basic ground rules are clear.

In this chapter, let's address these two tasks and get them out of the way.

The Warm-up

The *Warm-up*, first of all. Our goal here is simply to get the interview off to a good start and to make sure the candidate feels good about being here. A bit of small talk is all that's needed. Keep it brief and try to make it sound *real* rather than *feigned* – that's the key thing.

'*Any trouble finding us?*' That's one way of doing it. It's real, it's brief, and it gets the job done.

'*Boy, that was some football match last night!*' This is *not* such a good idea. For one thing, it sounds awfully corny. For another, you have no way of knowing whether the candidate *watched* the football match or even has any *interest* in football matches. Thirdly, if the candidate *did* see the football match and was absolutely *enthralled* by it, you might have trouble bringing this little bit of small talk to a close.

It's better to keep it brief. '*Any trouble finding us?*'

> Our goal is simply to get the interview off to a good start
> and to make sure the candidate feels good about being
> here.

The ground rules

*'Susan, I asked you to come in today because, as you know, we
have a vacancy and I'm responsible for filling it. I saw some things
in your CV that suggested an exploratory interview might be well
worth while.'*

This is good. You're saying something complimentary,
which will further the goal of putting Susan at ease, and you're
getting the basic facts of the situation out on the table. There's
a job to be filled and you're the manager whose responsibility
it is to fill it.

You're also saying that this is an *exploratory* interview, and
that's something that should be made clear. It is usually helpful
to go a step further and say something like:

*'I think our goal today, Susan, should be to see whether we want
to move ahead beyond this first interview. If things look good from
both your standpoint and mine, then we'll want to get together
again and explore things in more depth. For today, our goal is
simply to decide whether there's enough of a match here to
warrant moving ahead.'*

That puts it plainly enough. This is a first interview and our
purpose is to do an initial exploration and make a go or no-go
decision about whether to move on to a second interview. Both
of us have to feel good about moving ahead.

Any questions? That's something you should add by way of
bringing this portion of the interview to a close and building a
bridge between it and what is to follow. It also gives the
candidate a chance to confirm that, yes, he or she has the same
understanding of what this get-together is all about.

Summary

In this chapter we have looked at the start of the interview itself. We
identified two preliminary tasks that must be dealt with at the outset

◆ First, we need a brief warm-up period to get the candidate relaxed.

◆ Second, we need to talk about the purpose of the interview. To establish the ground rules.

CHAPTER 9

The Tools We'll Be Using

W e've engaged in a bit of small talk to help put Susan at ease and get the interview off to a positive start. We've also taken a minute or two to make sure that the goal of the interview – and its place in the total selection process – is clear on both sides. Now we begin the interview proper. And this, we agreed, will involve our talking about the following broad aspects of the candidate's background: education, work history, career goals and aspirations, this job and this company, and personal life and hobbies. Those are the areas that we are going to cover. That's our *plan*.

Before putting that plan into effect, let's make sure that we have our tools properly sharpened. There are three main tools that we will be using as we work through each main segment of the interview.

Getting the candidate to talk

The purpose of the interview is to gather information about the candidate. Information that goes beyond what we have already gleaned from the CV.

And the easiest and most direct way to gather information from someone is to ask a question.

In this chapter, we're going to look at *what* questions to ask, and at *how* to ask them. We're going to begin our discussion of the actual selection interview.

Let the candidate's 'personality' express itself

Remember, we're going to be looking for the behavioural patterns which were there in the past and will continue to be there in the future...what we've been calling the candidate's *personality*. That's what's going to allow us to predict his or her future performance.

How we organise the interview, and how we ask questions,

has to allow for that to happen. If we control things too tightly, there'll be little room for the candidate's 'personality' to express itself. On the other hand, if we leave things totally unstructured, we might not cover all the ground that needs to be covered.

Encourage the candidate to talk

Our manner of conducting the interview, and especially our manner of posing questions, has to be such that the candidate is encouraged to talk.

The candidate is probably a wee bit nervous to begin with, and certainly anxious to make a good impression. We'll have to overcome that, and we'll have to handle things in a manner that *brings out* the candidate's personality rather than causing it to be hidden behind a defensive shell.

The Lead-in

The first tool is the *Lead-in*. The *Lead-in* is an open-ended question that we use to move into each major segment of the interview – Education, for example – or to introduce a new subject within one segment. It *leads* the candidate into the area.

'*I see you've been with the Post Office for the past four years....could you tell me a little bit about the sort of work you've been doing?*'

> The Lead-in is an open-ended question that we use to move into each major segment of the interview.

This is what's known as an *open-ended* question. It is open-ended in that it directs the conversation into a pre-defined area without giving the candidate too much guidance as to what to discuss within that area or what we are looking for. It encourages them to tackle the area in whatever way they see fit. *Here's a topic*, in effect it says, *run with it.*

It may not even be a question.

'*Okay, George, your last job was with Consolidated Rubber... let's talk about that.*'

Or

'Tell me a little bit, if you could Linda, about what you are looking for at this stage in your career . . .'

It's a good idea to have a specific *Lead-in* for each major segment of the interview. That allows you to engineer a smooth transition from each one to the next. You don't have to memorise these questions. If you do, they'll probably come out sounding somewhat stilted and artificial. But you will find yourself asking them in a rather consistent fashion – and yet still being spontaneous – as you go along.

> It's a good idea to have a specific *Lead-in* for each major segment of the interview.

There are two rules to keep in mind:

♦ First, keep the Lead-in *open ended*. Don't move into a new subject area by asking a specific question.
♦ Second, after asking the Lead-in question, let the candidate talk. Don't interrupt.

If you open with a specific question rather than a general invitation to talk – or if you *interrupt* by introducing a specific question – you'll have to follow up with another one, and then another one after that. You, not the candidate, will carry the burden of keeping the conversation going.

The other thing that happens is that you lose a valuable opportunity to see the candidate 'at work'. When you throw the candidate an open-ended, unstructured invitation to talk about this or that general subject area, you're giving him or her a *problem to solve*. It's a good opportunity to see how they handle things:

♦ Do they get flustered, and ask you for more direction? Do they handle it smoothly, and display lots of poise?
♦ Do they stop to think a bit, and plan their overall approach, before getting started?
♦ Do they ramble on – to the point where you have to move in?
♦ Do they get bogged down in excessive detail?

The Probe

Our second main tool is called the *Probe*. When we want more detail, we *probe* for it. The *Probe* picks upon something the candidate has said – and probes for specifics. It generally starts with *what, who, when, why,* or *how* and it conveys a very simple message: *Tell me more.*

◆ *'Did he give you a reason for his decision?'*
◆ *'What happened when the group met again the following week?'*
◆ *'Is that all he said?'*

> The *Probe* picks upon something the candidate has said – and probes for specifics.

Probes don't have to be questions.

'Tell me a little bit more – if you could, John – about why you left.'

That's a *probe*, but it's expressed in the form of a mild directive rather than an actual question. Here's another example:

'Give me an example, Jacques, of the sort of problems you had to handle as Marketing Manager.'

It's important not to be too obvious or too aggressive in our probing. *'What did you say then? How did he react?'* Delivered in the wrong tone, blunt questions like these can easily imply a belligerence that you may or may not want to have conveyed. It's a lot better to simply show some genuine interest.

◆ *Just out of curiosity, Mike, what did you tell him when you saw him at the airport the next day?*
◆ *Now how on earth did you explain that to him?*

Show the candidate that you're getting involved, that you're anxious to hear the full story, that you're eager to find out exactly what happened.

It's a good idea, in fact, to *vary* the way in which you probe. There are times, for example, when a *statement* can serve as an effective probe.

'I bet that took some doing…getting him to change his mind, I mean.'

That's a statement rather than a question, but it clearly invited the candidate to tell us more.

Sometimes, our probe will take the form of what's usually known as a *reflective* statement, one that reflects back what the candidate has said.

*So you felt that the meeting would be a waste of time if the CEO
wasn't going to be there.*

In effect, we're asking the candidate to confirm that we have
understood correctly or drawn the right conclusion, or to
correct us if we're a bit off base. In either case, we normally get
some sort of elaboration.

Sometimes, we don't even need to use *words*. Just a *gesture*
will do. A raised eyebrow, a cocking of the head to one side, a
widening of the eyes...any little gesture that tells the person not
to skip ahead too quickly, we'd like to know more. Gestures of
this sort indicate that we are *reacting* to something the candidate
has said and that we want to go back and examine it.

The Follow-up

Our third main tool is the *Follow-up*. The *Follow-up* is a question
that we use to get at specific things that the candidate has not
talked about spontaneously in response to our initial *Lead-in*.

At some point, the candidate will begin winding down his
or her discussion of the subject. At that point, you either move
smoothly on to the next area – using another *Lead-in* – or else
stay in the area you're in and ask a *Follow-up* question.

The *Follow-up* is a question we insert into the discussion to
fill in the blanks – when there is a specific topic that we want
the candidate to talk about and they haven't got into it
spontaneously. The topic is too important to *skip*, so we *force* it
by asking a *Follow-up* question.

> The *Follow-up* is a question we insert into the discussion
> to fill in the blanks.

Let's say, for example, that we are talking with a candidate
named Jim and have moved into the area of his education. We
got into it by using a general *Lead-in* that simply asked Jim to
talk to us about his educational background. Then we let Jim
talk. Now...he's winding down his discussion, and seems to be
waiting for us to guide him into the next area. But he hasn't
told us which subject he enjoyed most at school, and why that

was. And that's something we want to know about. So, before moving on to the next area, we issue a *Follow-up* question.

'Of all the subjects which you studied, Jim, which one did you enjoy the most?'

Here are some other examples of *Follow-up* questions that you might wish to use:

- *If you could go back and do your college years over again, is there anything you'd change or do differently?*
- *When I started my first full-time job, I don't remember having any specific career goals in mind. How about you?*
- *What were some of the things that you particularly enjoyed about working for Carlton?*
- *Looking back on it now, how do you feel about the way your career has unfolded. Is it the 'real' you?*
- *How do you organise your day? When you get up in the morning, do you have a pretty good idea of what lies ahead?*

Note that these *Follow-up* questions are a bit more specific than the open-ended *Lead-in* that you use to start off each segment of the interview. But they're not *too* specific. They're not yes-or-no questions. They're not asking for a specific piece of information. Like the *Lead-in*, they are an invitation to talk. All we've done is narrow down the boundaries a bit.

Developing a 'my favourites' list

It's a good idea to have a set of *Follow-up* questions for each of the five main interview segments. These will be questions, by and large, which you develop yourself, based on your own experience, which you ask in every interview you conduct, and which have been chosen for their potency in stimulating discussion and eliciting useful information.

The important thing is that they be asked routinely in every interview. The more they're asked the more answers you get and the more you can begin to really *interpret* what you hear.

> It's a good idea to have a set of *Follow-up* questions for each of the five main interview segments.

You begin to see patterns in the answers you are given and you begin to see how certain types of responses are indicative of certain types of people and certain types of performance.

As we work through the next five chapters, covering the five major segments of the interview, we'll be introducing some

> The questions have to *sound* like you, and they have to be presented in a natural, almost conversational fashion.

good *Follow-ups* that you may wish to include in your own list of favourites. You will probably want to 'translate' them into your own terms and your own manner of speaking. The questions have to *sound* like you, and they have to be presented in a natural, almost conversational fashion. Develop a list with which you feel comfortable. Have it typed so that you can keep it in front of you when you are interviewing. Do this until the questions have become so familiar that they flow naturally and spontaneously, with no need on your part to refer to a written guide.

In the actual interview itself, you might even adapt them to suit the specific candidate you are dealing with. Some candidates respond best when you keep things businesslike and to the point. Others will react better to a more personal and conversational style. Some candidates don't mind a pointed question or a mild challenge. Others will be intimidated by it.

The tools at work – two examples

Let's look at two examples of our interviewing tools at work. We'll start by listening in on an interview with a chap named George.

George – training courses

Okay – we've got three tools. *The Lead-in. The Probe. The Follow-up.* Let's look at how these tools work together in an actual interview situation. We are talking with George, and we want to spend a bit of time talking about the various courses and seminars that he has taken. How much did he actually learn? How relevant are they? Is the fact that he took them a sign of initiative on his part?

We steer George into the subject by issuing a *Lead-in*:

*'I notice on your CV, George, that you've taken quite a few
courses over the years...'*

That's probably all we have to say. It's enough to let George
know what we want him to talk about.

As George talks, we listen carefully and *show* – by the
occasional nod or smile or raised eyebrow – that we are
listening. And, from time to time, we use a *Probe* to clarify a
point or press for more detail.

- *Three days seems like a lot. What was covered?*
- *I take it, then, that every new hire went through the exact same
two-week process?*
- *You've got a course here called 'Fuzzy Logic for Straight
Thinkers'. That sounds interesting...*

At some point, the conversation will wind down. George
stops talking and waits for us to indicate where we go from
here. At that point, if there are still some unanswered questions
in our mind regarding the courses which George has taken, we
throw out some relatively specific *Follow-ups*:

- *Looking back now, which of these courses do you think has had
the most impact on your performance?*
- *Are there specific things that you have been working on during
the past year?*
- *I'm curious about the course on Project Management. Is that one
that you chose yourself?*
- *Besides the courses that you've taken, are there other ways in
which you have worked to up-grade your skills?*
- *If you were designing a training course for yourself right now,
what are the things you would include? Why is that?*

Francine – dealing with setbacks

Let's look at another example of how the *Lead-ins*, *Probes*, and
Follow-ups work together in an actual interview.

The candidate is Francine. We've had a good discussion and
there's one last area we want to get into. How does she handle
setbacks and problems? We begin with a *Lead-in*:

*'I suppose we've all had our share of setbacks, Francine. Thinking
back over the past six months, what has been your biggest*

When is a question a *Lead-in* and when is it a *Follow-up*? When used to open a major segment of the interview – Work History, for example – it is clearly a *Lead-in*. An example:

◆ *'Let's talk now about your work experience, Judy. Could we start with your time at M&S?'*

A subsequent question which follows quite directly from a *Lead-in* is best referred to as a *Follow-up* simply because the term fits and it sounds right:

◆ *'When you first started with M&S, what were your specific responsibilities?'*

That's a *Follow-up* . . . a fill-in-the-blanks question that we use to get us into a specific area within the general *Work History* segment which the candidate has not got into.

But there are times when a question will represent such a break with what has gone before – even though we are staying within the same segment – that it seems most natural to call it a *Lead-in*:

◆ *'Work seems very important to you, Nick. You're not a closet workaholic, by any chance, are you?'*

◆ *'Let's talk about management style, Diane. How would you characterise your own approach?'*

◆ *'Judy, as you look back on your career as a whole, what assignment has been most satisfying to you?'*

These are all 'Work History' questions in the sense that they will come within that segment of the interview. But they introduce whole new subject areas rather than following up on something that has come before. Again, it seems more *natural* to refer to them as *Lead-ins*.

Fig. 3. Lead-ins versus Follow-ups.

disappointment?'

Let's assume that Francine comes back with an answer that's too general to really tell us anything:

'I suppose it's the fact that I have not achieved every single target that I set out to achieve . . . I tend to be quite hard on myself . . .'

That doesn't tell us very much, and it seems a wee bit self-serving. We need to go back and repeat the *Lead-in*, this time elaborating a bit so that Francine knows what we're after.

'Could we take one specific target and talk about it . . . a specific goal that was important to you and where you really felt disappointed when it was not achieved?'

Hopefully, that will be enough to get her on track. And, as

she talks, we inject the occasional *Probe* to clarify a point or dig for specifics:

- *Was this a new customer, or someone you had called on before?*
- *When the news came through that they had gone with the other firm, what was your reaction?*
- *How exactly did you say that?*
- *I don't quite understand why you felt he was hedging...*
- *Is that something you know for a fact – or is it more of an assumption you're making?'*

And we'll use occasional *Follow-up* questions to get at specific points that we want Francine to address:

- *Thinking now about what you were hoping to achieve, do you feel it was realistic?*
- *What caused them to go with the competition, Francine? Why do you think it happened?*
- *Could it have been avoided? Is there anything you could have done about it?*
- *Looking back on it now, are there specific things that you would change about your approach?*

Go easy on the questions

Even when the questions you are asking are unstructured ones, you should avoid asking *too many* questions. The interview should be more than a question-and-answer session. An experienced interviewer generally lets the candidate do most of the talking, using questions sparingly and asking them in an adroit manner that steers the flow of the conversation without intruding on it. The most important task is to encourage the candidate to talk openly and freely.

Your aim should be to ask questions that result in the candidate doing most of the talking. Specifically, if you find yourself doing more than 25 per cent of the talking, then your manner of phrasing questions will have to be looked at and adjusted.

Too heavy a reliance on the question as a means of stimulating conversation can result in a number of problems:

- The candidate may become defensive.
- Less information will be forthcoming.

◆ It places a burden on the interviewer.

The candidate may become defensive

When questioning is used in inquisitionary fashion, to take the extreme case, what results can hardly be called a 'conversation'. Even under the best of circumstances, too much questioning tends to arouse caution in the applicant. The fact that the interviewer has asked a question always implies that the subject matter is important – and the candidate cannot help but tread carefully when formulating a response.

Less information will be forthcoming

The more questions asked, ironically, the less information is obtained. The interviewer who asks one short question after another is going to be given one short response after another. And the responses, moreover, will get shorter and shorter as the interview proceeds.

When we ask too many questions, we are saying, in effect, 'If I want to know something, I'll ask you.' And this cannot help but impede the flow of genuine conversation.

It places a burden on the interviewer

Once an interview has deteriorated into a question-and-answer session, it is difficult to break the pattern. The onus is clearly on the interviewer to ask the questions, and the applicant's duty is simply to respond to each one as it is presented.

Under such conditions, the interviewer has little time to really think about what the candidate is saying – or even to listen carefully. He or she is too busy thinking about what question to ask next.

Summary

In this chapter we have considered what happens after the preliminaries of the interview and what tools we'll be using to make the most of the process.

First, some objectives:

◆ It is essential we get the candidate to talk freely.

◆ Let the candidate's personality express itself.

The three main tools we use are:

♦ The Lead-in questions.

♦ The Probe questions.

♦ The Follow-up questions. It's important here to have a set of Follow-up questions you can easily refer to and that you're quite comfortable with.

♦ Remember a *Lead-in* question starts that phase of the interview and a *Follow-up* question helps to develop or enlarge upon that phase.

Don't let the questioning get too heavy:

♦ Remember to give the candidate time to talk.

♦ The candidate may become defensive if you use questions alone to elicit discussion.

♦ Less information will be forthcoming.

♦ It places a burden on you, the interviewer, and you may miss some of the behavioural patterns you set out to identify.

Let's work through the five main segments of the interview. We'll start with education.

Area 1 – Education

There are two things going on in every interview. On the one hand, you and the candidate are *talking* about things. You're covering certain ground, spending time on certain topics. That's the *content* of the interview. That's what an outsider would hear if they tuned in.

But there's something *else* happening during the interview. You're assessing what the candidate has to offer. You're drawing up and testing out hypotheses about the sort of person he or she is and about whether he or she has the make-up needed to be a top performer. This is the *mental* side of the interview. It goes on inside your head.

These two processes go on simultaneously. The content of the interview, on the one hand, is divided into five main segments, starting with education and proceeding through to personal life and hobbies.

1. Education.

2. Work History.

3. Career Goals and Aspirations.

4. This Specific Opportunity.

5. Personal Life and Hobbies.

Your assessment of what the candidate has to offer, on the other hand, is spread across the twelve factors which make up *The Winner's Profile*.

Five areas, twelve factors. Five areas in terms of the content of the interview. Twelve qualities in terms of how we assess the candidate.

Segments first

Because the actual *conduct* of the interview – what we talk about – has to be organised around the five *Areas* we outlined rather than the twelve *Factors* we are trying to assess, it is easier to review the *Areas* first.

We need to use the five Areas in a way that sheds light on the candidate through the twelve Factors that we want to assess. That's the key logistical challenge of the interview.

On the pages which follow, we will be going through each of the five areas in some detail. We'll start with a *Lead-in* to get us into the area and then look at some good *Follow-ups* which help us dig for the information we need. And we will be quite precise about the information we are after.

> We need to go through the five Areas and talk in a way that sheds light on the candidate in terms of the twelve Factors that we want to assess.

The Lead-in

Let's start with education. We'll have a sketchy outline of Susan's educational background from the CV. Our purpose in the interview is to flesh out some of the details and to press for a glimpse of the *person* behind the education.

We begin with a *Lead-in*:

'Let's talk for a while, Susan, about your educational background. I see from your CV that... – and here we can add on something such as *you did your undergraduate work in the United States* or *you went to Peterborough...that's where I went, too.'*

The key thing is that the *Lead-in* tells the candidate clearly what general area we want to talk about, but it gives her – Susan – lots of leeway to do so in whatever way she chooses.

And then we let Susan talk. As she talks, we use *Probes* to get at the details – the *whys* and the *hows* – and *Follow-ups* to get at specific aspects of Susan's educational background that she might not talk about in response to our general *Lead-in*.

The key thing is this. Our *Probes* and *Follow-ups* should be used to get at information that is going to be relevant – and 'relevant' means that it will help us assess Susan on the twelve dimensions that we have targeted. When we dig for information, there should be a reason for doing so.

Let's go through the specific *Factors* – starting with *Goal Orientation* – upon which we can expect to shed some light during our discussion of Susan's education. In each case, we'll start by suggesting some good *Follow-up* questions that you might wish to use and then turn our attention to what you can learn from the answers you get.

> When we dig for information, there should be a reason for doing so.

Goal Orientation

We ask ourselves the question: Did Susan have a *goal* for herself? Did she know what she was trying to achieve and why she wanted to achieve it? Did she have a specific career objective at that stage in her life, and were her educational choices made with that longer-term goal in mind?

◆ *When you decided to go to college, what specific vocational plans or goals did you have in mind?*

◆ *I'm not sure I really had a clear goal for myself when I decided to go to university. How about you?*

◆ *I see you chose mathematics as your main subject. Do you recall how that decision was made?*

Give high marks to the candidate whose education was consciously designed and chosen to fit into a longer-term career plan which was realistic at the time and which has been successfully executed.

Organisation

'*That was a pretty heavy workload – taking four courses and holding down a part-time job at the same time. How did you manage?*'

Look for signs that Susan tackled her educational goals in the same way that our top people tackle their *work* goals – in a focused, systematic, disciplined manner. The important thing is to probe for specifics in regard to how Susan went about things. How she planned her work, prepared for exams, carried out major projects, and managed her time. Are there signs that she was constantly scrambling, having to study all night in order to get ready for an exam which had been scheduled for months. Was she having trouble juggling all the priorities on her agenda? Or was she able to pace herself, tackle first things first, and get everything done?

Intelligence

- *How hard did you have to work in order to get the marks you did – compared to the other students in your class?*
- *How many hours per week would you say that you worked on the various subjects you were taking?*
- *I see from your CV that you went into the first year at Peterborough on an undergraduate scholarship...*

The sheer *content* of a person's education sometimes gives us at least a general measure of how much *Intelligence* they will bring to the job. It really boils down to three critical questions:

- How difficult were the courses they took?
- How well did they do?
- How hard did they have to work?

And – has Susan made intelligent choices in regard to her education? Sometimes, a quick *Probe* is all that's needed to dig for the information we need.

Susan: *'I spent five, maybe six months in Europe, and then I came back in time to enrol for the September term at Queen's.'*

You: *'Why Queens?'*

Why was the decision made? Was it thought through carefully? Part of being a successful person is making intelligent choices that will best help us get to where we are trying to get to. Finding out about *why* a candidate has made critical decisions – going to this university rather than that university, working for this company rather than that company – tells us a great deal about how astutely they weigh options and arrive at a decision. And that is an important part of what we have called the *Intelligence* factor.

Relationship-Building

We are looking for signs that Susan built friendships during her university years – friendships which have endured through to the present.

♦ *During the four years you were at Peterborough, did you get involved in any extracurricular activities?*

♦ *Have you been able to keep in touch with either of these people during the time since you all graduated?*

Some people get so wrapped up in their studies that they don't really do much mixing. They don't get involved in things. Other people do mix and socialise, and they do develop friendships, but those friendships don't run deep enough to last beyond the university years. Give high marks to a candidate who not only worked hard and did well at university, but who also found time to get involved in things and build some friendships which have stood the test of time.

Drive

Ask yourself, as Susan talks about her education, whether she had to make any tough choices – any sacrifices – in order to achieve her educational goals.

Did she work her way through university? That's one question that might give us some clues. If Susan had to work her way through university, giving up some of the leisure time that her friends might have been enjoying, then it tells us something about her level of *Drive*. It tells us that she didn't just have goals... she was *committed* to them, enough to give up something in the process of working toward them.

♦ *How was your education financed? Did you have to carry most of the burden yourself?*

♦ *You had to leave Kent and head north in order to get into university... Was that a difficult decision?*

♦ *Five years is a long grind. Was there any point where you got discouraged, where you felt like throwing in the towel?*

Being committed, making tough choices, making sacrifices, working hard to get where one wants to go, staying focused... these are all part and parcel of the *Drive* factor.

Stayability

Does the candidate have a basic affinity for the types of products and customers which are inherent in the opportunity for which he or she is being considered? Sometimes, our discussion of the candidate's educational background can give us some clues.

- *Which subjects did you enjoy most while you were at Peterborough? Why was that?*
- *Which subjects did you find the least enjoyable? What was there about them that you didn't enjoy?*
- *Which were the subjects in which you received your best grades? Why do you think that was?*
- *Which subjects did you do less well in? Why do you think that was?*

If it turns out that Susan positively *hated* chemistry and biology and anything else that smacked of the 'hard' sciences, then we might have to wonder how much she would enjoy dealing with a highly engineered product or working in a fundamentally *technical* area of the company. It would not be a *knockout punch*, obviously – just a cause for concern. Something to probe for at other points in the interview.

Keep it brief

If the candidate is a recent graduate, you will probably want to spend a considerable amount of time exploring their education. There may be times when a candidate doesn't have any work experience to speak of, in fact, and in that case the bulk of the interview might well be spent on the subject of their education.

With most candidates, however, you should not be spending a great deal of time reviewing their educational background. It is instructive, yes. But it is even *more* instructive to look at their work experience. The personal qualities which can be assessed in our discussion of the candidate's education – *Goal Orientation*, for example – can be equally well and usually better assessed once we move on to the next of our five interview segments.

Still, there is good information to be gleaned even in this early portion of the interview.

> We should be digging, and thinking, and drawing up tentative hypotheses about what certain facts tell us about the candidate.

The fact that Susan did well in chemistry but not in sociology may mean that she doesn't do well with 'intangibles'. The fact that she followed a friend's example by going to this or that specific college and then, between terms, went to work in her father's business, may indicate a lack of independence. But – it may not. We have to do this sort of thinking, but we have to remember that we are generating *hypotheses* that will need to be checked.

Summary

In this chapter we established that the content of the interview is divided into five main segments and we concentrated on the first – Education. We also explained how we apply our assessment of what each candidate has to offer through the twelve factors comprising the Winner's Profile against each of these segments.

The five segments are:

- ◆ Education.
- ◆ Work History.
- ◆ Career Goals and Aspirations.
- ◆ This Specific Opportunity.
- ◆ Personal Life and Hobbies.

The Education segment questions could be based on some of the twelve factors from the Winner's Profile:

- ◆ The *Lead-in* could refer to something on the CV.
- ◆ *Goal Orientation* asks what vocational goals did the candidate have in mind when deciding upon a course or a college.
- ◆ *Organisation* would seek answers to how the candidate coped with the workload.
- ◆ *Intelligence* would enquire how difficult the candidate found the course to be.
- ◆ *Relationship-building* would ask about extracurricular activities.
- ◆ *Drive* – how was your education financed?
- ◆ *Stayability* would ask which subjects the candidate did well in and which were less successful. *Why?*

◆ Remember not to spend too much time on the Education segment.

◆ All the time you should be digging and thinking. Drawing a picture in your mind about what the candidate's behaviour is telling you.

This is a key
segment in the
interview
process – a
chronological
look at the
candidate's
career to date.

CHAPTER 11

Area 2 – Work History

N ow, let's move into the next segment of the interview –
our discussion of the candidate's *Work History*.

You can do it in one of two ways. One is to start with the
person's current or most recent position and then work
backward in time from there, spending less and less time on
each job as you move further and further into the past. The
other way is to do it in chronological order, starting with what
they did when they left school and working toward the present.

Let's do it chronologically. Here is a *Lead-in* to get this
portion of the interview started:

*'What I would like to do now, Susan, is go through your career,
one step at a time, looking at what was involved in each step
along the way. Let's go right back to when you left school. On
your CV, you indicate that you worked for two years at Post Office
Counters...'*

That's all we need to do – let her know that we want to review
her career step by step and that we want to proceed
chronologically.

It's a good idea to have Susan's CV in front of you as she
talks. It helps you follow along and keep the dates straight. You
may also want to probe for more detail in regard to specific
achievements or pieces of information which she has included.

> Have the candidate's CV in front of you as they talk.

As your discussion with Susan touches upon each of the
jobs she has had during her career to date, there are basic
questions you have to keep in mind:

◆ *How and why did she take the job?*
◆ *What was the job all about?*
◆ *What specific challenges or problems did she have to face?*
◆ *How well did she perform?*
◆ *Why did she leave?*

Let's go through the specific *factors* which we will be looking at during this segment of the interview.

Goal Orientation

In assessing whether Susan is a *goal-oriented* sort of person, we look in her work history for signs that she has managed her career in a goal-oriented fashion and set personal performance goals for herself in each of the jobs she has held.

◆ *I'm curious about your reasons for moving over into the marketing area...*

◆ *When you went into that job, did you have any specific personal targets that you were aiming for?*

Choices, again, are revealing. Careers are shaped by the choices a person makes, and what we look for here is evidence that Susan's choices were part of a game plan that she had for herself... that they helped move her toward the accomplishment of longer-term career goals which she had set for herself. It boils down to specifics – why she moved over into the marketing area, for example.

Organisation

It is always instructive to talk about how a candidate has tackled a major project.

'It says on your CV that you put a new telemarketing programme in place. Could you tell me a bit more about just what was involved?'

We're using introducing a telemarketing programme as an example, but it could be anything. Re-vamping the order desk, writing a key proposal, putting together a one-off newsletter, finding ways to reduce courier expenses or organising a seminar or sales presentation.

As Susan talks, probe for specifics.

◆ Did she start by clarifying goals and deadlines, thinking through the overall strategy, and putting together a step-by-step action plan?

◆ Did she use a critical path approach, with specific dates attached to each step?

- Was she realistic in her estimates of how long various things would take?
- Did she make full use of the resources around her?
- Did she get other people involved when appropriate?
- Did she consult with people who would be affected by the project or who were intended to be its beneficiaries?

'How do you normally plan or organise your day? Yesterday, for example...'

It's always interesting, and revealing, to ask people to talk about how they plan their day. It's one of those areas, first of all, that most candidates are not *expecting* to have to talk about – so you get fewer tiresome, rehearsed answers.

It's a crucial area, too, because it gets to the heart of what good performance in *any* job is all about. Outstanding annual results, the building of long-term customer relationships, the meeting and surpassing of monthly quotas...all of these things are achieved *one day at a time*.

The importance of time planning

Good performers know that. They've learned to treat time as a precious commodity that can't be wasted. They know they aren't going to get everything done, so they've learned to distinguish very clearly between what's important and what's not important.

Look for evidence that Susan is doing more than just listing the 'things to do' for the next day. Look for evidence that she is allocating time in accordance with some sort of broader strategy: this percentage for telephone work, that percentage for staff meetings, and so on.

Look for evidence that she can distinguish between what's urgent and what's important. Self-development, for example, is one of those things which almost all of us recognise as being important...but it's never *urgent*. So it hardly ever actually gets put on our schedule.

Effective performers don't just prioritise what's on their schedule; they schedule their priorities.

> Look for evidence that she can distinguish between what's urgent and what's important.

Initiative

If Susan is the sort of person with *Initiative*, it's most likely to show up in our discussion of her work history. But we'll have to dig for it, using our *Probe* and *Follow-up* tools. *Initiative* is one of those qualities that we can assess only by looking at the detail of what was going on in a situation, what went through the candidate's mind, what other people were doing at the time, what pressures were at work or had to be responded to, what the candidate actually *did*, and how long it took him or her to do it.

'You said the meeting had to be cancelled, Susan, and you re-scheduled it for the next afternoon. Was that pretty straightforward? Around here, I mean, it's almost impossible to schedule a meeting unless you give everyone at least a week's notice...'

That's a *Probe*. We classify it as a *Probe* because it follows on the heels of something that Susan has said – a seemingly innocuous statement about having to reschedule a meeting.

If we dig for the details, it might turn out that re-scheduling the meeting for the next afternoon was, indeed, a fairly straightforward matter. But it might *also* turn out that this is a glorious example of *Initiative*. The meeting had to be cancelled and the next regularly scheduled meeting was not until the same day of the following week. But Susan decided that the meeting was critical so she got on the phone and spent the whole morning getting things arranged so that all of the key people except two could be there at four o'clock the next day. In the process, she had to spend five minutes persuading Allan that *her* meeting was more crucial that the product development meeting that he was scheduled to attend –

'You know how listless those meetings are, Allan...give yourself a break and come to a meeting where some real sparks are going to fly!' –

and she had to arrange for Francine to sit in for Jacques at the Basingstoke conference and for Jill's proposal to be sent down by courier rather than hand-delivered by Jill herself.

That's *Initiative*. And that's the kind of behaviour that we see day in and day out in our top performers.

Intelligence

How difficult was the job that Susan was doing? How much learning was involved? How complex was the material she had to master? Was it a job where she had to think quickly on her feet and decide how to handle things? Was there a lot of high-level analysis involved in her work?

◆ *Tell me a bit about the up-front training you received. What exactly was involved?*

◆ *Tell me briefly about the product, Susan. What sort of microscopes are we talking about here?*

◆ *It seems to me, in that sort of job, that you'd have to be pretty quick on your feet... Am I reading things correctly?*

◆ *Okay, you got the data from the accounting people. Then what happened? Was it you who actually did the analysis?*

The answers to all of these questions give us clues as to how intelligent Susan is. We don't need to know *precisely* how intelligent she is. We don't need to estimate her *IQ*. What's important is that we come away feeling confident that she has the solid, practical, above-average intelligence needed to both master the job and do it effectively on a day-to-day basis.

Relationship-building

Look for signs that Susan has worked well with people... that she has been a good team player, built good relationships with people in other departments, got to know her colleagues on something a bit more than just a business basis, played an active role in committees and groups or been involved in special industry groups or professional associations. These are all signs of a person who works *with* people and takes active steps to build relationships.

◆ *If you seem to have got along well with the people in the Marketing area...*

◆ *On the order desk, were calls from that same customer always routed through to the same person? Is that the way it worked?*

If Susan has had Order Desk or Customer Service experience, for example, probe for signs – as we do in the question above – of her having worked closely enough with customers to build a *relationship* with them, even if it was only done over the telephone.

Leadership

Susan's work history is a good place to be looking for signs of *Leadership*.

- *Was everyone in the group thinking along those same lines, or did you have to do a bit of arm-twisting?*
- *You say you got the committee's approval to do a newsletter. Was that difficult? Did they have to be persuaded?*
- *On those occasions when you needed the marketing research people involved, how did you arrange for that?*

Getting the boss to go along with an idea, getting the committee to give the go-ahead for a special newsletter, going to the people in marketing research and pulling them into a project...these are all things which might well give us a glimpse of Susan the *Leader* in action. Or, they might not. We have to probe for the specifics.

Self-development

It is in our discussion of Susan's work history that we begin to look for evidence that she is someone who believes in and practises *Self-development*.

- *What did you learn in that job? In what ways do you feel you developed during those two years?*
- *You went into that job without a great deal of experience... What did you do to bring yourself up to speed?*

We need to look beyond the training and coursework which was built into her job – which were automatically given to or expected of anyone in the job – and delve into what she did *on her own accord* to enhance her own performance potential.

We can also ask candidates to talk not so much about what they had to learn in a specific job but about what they have learned *generally* during the past year or so:

- *What are some of the specific things you have been working on during the past year or two?*
- *With what results?*

- *How do you assess that? How do you gauge whether you've actually changed?*
- *In what specific ways do you feel you have changed or developed during the past year or two?*
- *Has that had a bearing on the results you've actually achieved in your job?*

Notice, in these examples, that our *Follow-ups* consist of a *series* of two or three questions rather than a single question – there are follow-ups to the follow-up, as it were. This is something that you'll see a lot in experienced interviewers. They ask a follow-up question, and then they ask a follow-up to the follow-up.

> We need to look beyond the training and coursework which were built into her job and delve into what she did on her own accord to enhance her own performance potential.

Stayability

In discussing Susan's career history, we have to pay special attention to the *Stayability* factor.

- *What were some of the things about that job that you especially liked or enjoyed?*
- *What were some of the things that you didn't like or found distasteful?*
- *What were some of the problems or frustrations you had to deal with?*

What does her previous career tell us about her probable reaction to the specific role which she is being considered for and to working within your organisation?

That's the question that we have to have tucked away in the back of our mind as we ask the more specific *Follow-up* questions listed above.

> What do Susan's past reactions tell us about her future reactions? Not just Susan's reactions but her *choices* as well.

- *You turned down Pitney Bowes and went with a small*

competitor. *Why was that?*

◆ *What sorts of things did you take into account in deciding to accept their offer?*

◆ *It says there that you left in April of the following year... What happened?'*

Why did Susan choose this job rather than that job? What was it about that sort of work that attracted her or led her to think it was the right type of work for her? What is it about this type of work that she enjoys the most?

Delve into these questions, and you'll learn a lot about the sort of environment that brings out the best in a candidate, the sort of climate they work best in, the sort of boss they work best for, the sort of people they like to work *with*.

How well did she perform?

One of the things we have not talked about up to this point is how well the candidate, Susan, has actually *performed* in the various jobs which she has done during the course of her career. It is an absolutely critical piece of information that we have to gather.

One way to find out is to just ask:

'Susan, looking back on the two years you spent in the Leeds branch, how would you assess your performance?'

Successful people focus on results, on contribution, and they keep track of how they are doing. Ask them how well they performed in a job, and what yardsticks they use to gauge that, and you will usually get a clear, specific answer.

> Successful people focus on results, on contribution, and they keep track of how they are doing.

Here are some additional ways to get at the question of how Susan performed.

◆ *How would you personally evaluate your performance in that job?*

◆ *How was your performance in that job evaluated by other people?*

◆ *If you could go back and do that job over again, are there things that you would do differently?*

Another way, of course, is to look for tangible signs of

above-average achievement – in the form of special awards, membership in the Achievers' Club, year-end bonuses, and the like. It is important to press for a bit of detail here. It might turn out that the year-end bonus, or even membership in the Achievers' Club, was pretty routine. Practically *everyone* got it.

And why did she leave?

How we raise this issue – how we actually phrase the question – will depend on what we've seen on the CV.

◆ *What were the principal reasons for your deciding to leave that job?*

◆ *You left Barclays after only a year-and-a-half... How exactly did that come about?*

◆ *It says here, Michael, that you left Tarmac because of 'limited advancement opportunities'. Could we talk a bit more about that?*

We sometimes get an indication of how well the candidate has performed when we find out – not just *discuss* but actually *find out* – the reasons for their leaving a job or company. This is one of those areas where it really pays to do some digging rather than accepting the candidate's initial response at face value.

Let's say, for example, that candidate Jeff Higgins said he was laid off due to a cutback in office personnel in the branch office where he had been working.

In these uncertain economic times, that seems to be an understandable enough reason to no longer be with the company.

But let's ask ourselves a question. If he was really good, would the company have let him go just like that? Wouldn't it have bent over backwards to try to relocate him with another branch? The chances are good that if he were *really* a top-notch performer, the company would have found a spot for him. Somewhere. Just so as not to lose him.

Check up on details

And was it really a cutback in personnel? How many people were let go, for example? Were they replaced? Were they all let go at the same time – or was this clearly an individual termination? Was there any discussion of *why* the company was deciding to let *him* go? How was the decision explained or announced to him? By whom?

If we dig deeply enough, there's at least an even chance that we'll find that the company was not happy with his performance. Or at least not happy enough to make any great effort to relocate him within the organisation.

But tread carefully here. Don't *assume* there's some sort of hidden reason for his job being terminated. Try not to be a cynic. But – if you have to choose between being a cynic who assumes that there is *always* a reason for someone being let go, and being someone who naively accepts things at face value and assumes that the person is telling the whole story... by all means go ahead and be a cynic.

Summary

In this chapter we have looked at the second segment – Work History – and agreed that this is one of the most important aspects of the interview process.

Throughout this part of the interview these questions should be kept in mind:

- How and why did the candidate take the job?
- What was the job all about?
- What specific challenges or problems did the candidate have to face?
- How well did the candidate perform?
- Why did the candidate leave?

The following questions from the Winner's Profile could apply to this segment:

- *Goal Orientation* would seek to identify what personal targets prompted the candidate's application for a particular job?
- *Organisation* – How did the candidate achieve results, claimed in their CV, whilst in that post?
- *Initiative* asks how the candidate overcame certain problems. The answers will depend upon probing questions.
- *Intelligence* would seek to make the link between

qualifications, training and performance.

- ◆ *Relationship-building* sets out to establish a behaviour of good interpersonal skills and team-building.
- ◆ *Leadership* seeks examples of persuasion and inspirational practice.
- ◆ *Self-development* is about gaining experience and how it affects performance.
- ◆ *Stayability* asks why the candidate stayed in a job for any particular period and what prompted their move.
- ◆ It's also worth considering at this point how well the candidate actually performed in the jobs covered to date. It all helps towards your picture of the candidate's behaviour.

CHAPTER 12

Area 3 – Career Goals and Aspirations

We now move on to the next area – the candidate's *Career Goals*.

There are two ways of looking at this area. The first is to address the issue of specific career goals and objectives. To talk about what Susan is looking for at this point in her career and where she would like to be at some point down the road.

The other is to talk more generally about the *ideal* job, the ideal boss, the ideal environment. If it turns out that Susan does not have specific career goals, she still ought to be able to talk coherently about what sort of job, what sort of boss, and what sort of work environment tend to bring out the best in her.

Let's start with the more specific issue of career goals and objectives. The *Lead-in*:

'Let's look now – if we could, Susan – at what you see lying ahead in your career and where you'd like to be five or so years down the road.'

Then we let Susan talk, and we listen.

One important note – don't be swayed too much by the candidate's outward *style* as they talk about this area. An experienced candidate will recognise the need to talk about career goals and aspirations, and will have taken time to put some thoughts together. A less experienced candidate may have to stop and think a bit. That doesn't necessarily mean that their aspirations are any less real. It *might*. But it might not.

Goal Orientation

We want to see that Susan has clear and specific goals for her career – that she knows exactly where she is going.

◆ *Where do you see yourself going from here? Where would you like to be five years from now, for example?*

◆ *Are there other options that you're looking at, or have you pretty well made up your mind about things?*

◆ *How did you set those goals? Did you actually sit down and think about them, and write them down?*

If she seems unclear or gives an answer that is rather general –

'I guess what I really want to do is continue doing what I do, because I enjoy it, and really feel that I've made a contribution to the company I am working for.'

we may want to use a Follow-up:

'Are there specific yardsticks or benchmarks that you would use to assess how your career is going? For some people, it's how much money they're making. Or being the number one performer on the team...'

Successful performers tend to have specific goals, not general ones.

Successful performers tend to have specific goals, not general ones. They know quite precisely where they are going and how they will know when they have arrived. If Susan seems vague about her goals, press for some specifics. If she has difficulty being more specific, stop pressing. If you press too hard, there's a good chance that she'll *invent* some goals right there on the spot just because you're so obviously looking for them.

Are Susan's goals realistic? That's another question we have to ask ourselves. Are they more or less in line with her capabilities? Could it be said that Susan is shooting too *low* – that her goals aren't challenging *enough*?

Stayability

Susan's answers to these Follow-ups may give us some important clues regarding the *Stayability* factor.

◆ *What are the things that are important to you in a job or in a company? Why?*

- ◆ *What are some of the things you would wish to avoid in a job or in a company?*
- ◆ *How would you describe the ideal boss? What sort of manager really brings out the best in you?*
- ◆ *Ignoring this particular opportunity for a minute, what are the specific things you're looking for at this stage in your career?*

Is what she is looking for compatible with what she is likely to *get*? That's the issue. Can we satisfy her needs? Are her goals realistically achievable within the time frame that she has in mind?

The basic question is this. Is what we're hearing from Susan consistent with what we know about the job for which she is being considered, the boss on whose team she will be working, and the environment in which that work will be done? How close is the overlap between what Susan considers ideal and what she is likely to experience if she joins us?

Summary

In this chapter we considered the third segment of Career Goals and Aspirations.

There are two ways of looking at this segment:

- ◆ The first is to address the issue of specific career goals and objectives.
- ◆ The second is to talk more generally about the *ideal* job, the ideal boss, the ideal environment.

- ◆ One of these should promote fruitful discussion.

The following questions from the Winner's Profile could apply to this segment:

- ◆ The *Lead-in* asks what the candidate sees lying ahead in their career.
- ◆ *Goal Orientation* is more specific – Where do you see yourself in five years time?
- ◆ *Stayability* would perhaps seek to establish those career criteria the candidate thinks to be important in a company to make them want to stay.

This job, this
organisation,
this climate –
and you as the
prospective
manager. What
are Susan's
thoughts?

CHAPTER 13

Area 4 – This Specific Opportunity

N ow we move into the fourth area to be covered during
our initial interview. We talk about *This Specific
Opportunity*. This job. This company. What does the candidate
think about the role under discussion. And what are their
thoughts about your company or organisation as an employer?

*'I'd like to talk now, Susan, about your view of this particular
opportunity. To start, do you have any basic questions about the
job?'*

At some point in the interview, we have to give Susan an
opportunity to ask questions about the job, and now is
probably a good time to do it. Remember what we said about
hiring being a two-way street . . . both sides have an important
decision to make.

Then, we ask *our* questions.

Self-development

There will be some sort of learning curve. There always is, even
when a person is moving across from the inside rather than
joining the organisation for the first time.

♦ *If you join us, obviously, you'll be dealing with a whole new
kind of customer . . . what sort of adjustments do you think
might be needed on your part?*

♦ *One of my concerns is that you haven't dealt with this complex
a product before. Any thoughts about that?*

♦ *Is there anything special that you've done to get ready for this
new assignment?*

Does she accurately recognise the slope and duration of
the learning curve?

So one of the questions we ask about Susan's perception of

This Opportunity is whether she accurately recognises the slope and duration of the learning curve and can be expected to meet the challenge in a positive and proactive manner. Has she taken steps to get ready? Has she gathered information about the job? Has she done a thorough assessment of the 'fit' between her own skills and the demands of the role? Has she, at the very least, sat down and *thought* about these issues?

Stayability

- *From where you stand, what do you see as the main challenges or difficulties in this job?*
- *I've talked about some of the challenges we're facing out in the field and some of the new directions we're taking... how do you see yourself making a contribution?*
- *Have you talked to your wife (husband) about this opportunity? How does she (he) feel about it?*
- *What appeals to you in this job that you have not had in your previous situation?*

This is an absolutely crucial area, and that's because a hiring decision has to work both ways. It has to give us – the company, and the manager doing the hiring – the very best person for the job. But it also has to give the *person* what they are looking for and what they *need*. It has to be a mutual decision. Two parties deciding to work together. It has to be a win-win situation that pays off for both sides.

And it is worth noting that what a candidate is looking for and what they *need* are not always the same thing. A candidate

> What a candidate is looking for and what they need are not always the same thing.

might want the job badly and see it as a logical next step in their career and be excited about being part of your organisation. But if they *need* a lot of direction, or *need* to be able to work at a relaxed pace and not have too many balls up in the air at one time, or *need* to be in a job where they can do their own thing and not have to take a lot of direction or follow a lot of rules, then they are not going to be successful in *this* job or in *this* company.

And people don't always *know* what they need. It's part of our job to find these things out and – having done that – take whatever course of action we feel is best *for both sides*. If the person's needs are not going to be met, no matter how badly they want the job or how enthusiastic they are, we *owe* it to both them and us to steer them away.

Comparing this to the ideal

It is often helpful to link the discussion of the ideal situation – in the Career Goals portion of the interview – to the discussion of this specific opportunity. For example:

Under Career Goals we asked...

◆ *Ignoring this particular opportunity for a minute, what are the specific things you're looking for at this stage in your career? Anything else?*

And now, under This Opportunity, we follow up with:

◆ *You've talked a while ago about some of the things you're looking for at this stage in your career...Do you think you'll find them here?*

Under Career Goals we asked...

◆ *Ignoring this particular opportunity, if you had to pick one company to work for, who would it be? Why is that?*

And now, under This Opportunity, we follow up with:

◆ *And a little while ago, you said that somewhere like ASDA or Tesco might be a good place to work...How would you think this company might compare to ASDA?*

Under Career Goals we asked...

◆ *How would you describe the ideal boss? What sort of manager really brings out the best in you?*

And now, under This Opportunity, we follow up with:

◆ *You described your ideal boss a bit earlier. What's your sense about the kind of boss you might have if you got this job?*

Summary

> In this chapter we have looked at the fourth segment entitled
> This Specific Opportunity

We can start this part of the procedure by:

> ◆ Seeking the candidate's *opinions* about the job and the
>   company.
>
> ◆ Letting the candidate also ask questions about *details* of the
>   job.

*The following questions from the Winner's Profile could apply to
this segment:*

> ◆ *Self-development* seeks to establish with the candidate what
>   they'll do to meet the demands of the job.
>
> ◆ *Stayability* asks what appeals to the candidate about this job
>   and what they would look for from the company to
>   encourage a successful working partnership.
>
> ◆ We can also link questions in this segment to answers given
>   in Career Goals discussions earlier in the interview.

*Finally, a look
at Susan the
person – social
and family life,
hobbies, and
general lifestyle.*

CHAPTER 14

Area 5 – Personal Life and Hobbies

The fifth and final segment of the first interview will be devoted to a discussion of the candidate's *Personal Life and Hobbies*. There's a lot to talk about here – current family situation, social activities, leisure-time pursuits, hobbies, general 'lifestyle' – but the discussion needn't be time-consuming. Try to zero in on the things that really tell you something meaningful about the person.

Goal Orientation

We look for signs that Susan has set goals for herself in regard to her hobbies. Not *all* of them. A lot of what a person does in their leisure time ought to be done for the sheer pleasure of doing it. One sign of a healthy, well-balanced person, after all, is that they know how to relax. Still, most people will have one, perhaps two hobbies which they take quite seriously and in regard to which the idea of setting specific goals is quite relevant. In such cases, we have another opportunity to assess the person as a goal-setter.

If it turns out that Susan has been studying the piano since the age of three, or has a butterfly collection, of if she happens to mention that she would like to learn a foreign language . . . does she, or *has* she, set goals? Are those goals specific? Are there target dates attached? Are the goals realistic and achievable? Are they *challenging* goals?

Organisation

It is always helpful to talk with candidates about how they *planned* something. A Christmas party, a school dance, a car boot sale, a special project at work, a conference, a training workshop, a holiday. Or it could be planning how to make the down payment on a new home, planning how to afford private schooling for the kids, planning how to get a small company off the ground.

♦ *I see on your CV that you founded a Girl Guides company in your community. That sounds like quite an achievement. Could you tell me a bit more about it?*

♦ *When you took the year off to travel to the Orient, what sort of planning went into it?*

> It is always helpful to talk with candidates about how they *planned* something.

When people talk about how they planned something, you'll get a glimpse of whether or not they set goals. You'll see whether they established an overall strategy and translated that strategy into a coherent action plan. You'll see whether their plan was based on an accurate estimate of how long things would take or how much things would cost.

Relationship-building

One of the things you can look for in discussing a candidate's background during this first interview is evidence of *sociability.* Look for evidence that the person chooses to be with people rather than doing things on his or her own. Are Susan's hobbies solitary, for example, or do they bring her into contact with other people? Does she belong to any clubs? Is she active in the community? Does she seem to watch a lot of television?

Drive

As we talk to Susan about her hobbies and leisure activities, we should be looking for signs that there is a competitive colouring to the things she enjoys the most – and that it is this competitive element, in fact, which makes these things so enjoyable.

♦ *You mentioned music as being one of your hobbies... could you tell me a bit more about that?*

And – how *intensely* is Susan involved in her major hobby, for example? Is it something she does as a lark, just to pass the time, or is it a serious pursuit into which she has put a lot of herself? Does she do something for a couple of months and then get bored with it, or has her hobby been a lifelong pursuit? Is it perhaps taken *too* seriously? If it's taken very seriously, what does she do for *fun*?

Stayability

In talking about the candidate's family and social life, finally, ask yourself – Is this *our* kind of person?

♦ *I see under Hobbies, on your CV, you've put 'Hell's Angels' ... I take it that's a club or community group of some sort ...*

We should ask this question with some degree of trepidation, but it's an important one. Someone who hangs out with motorcycle gangs may not be quite this company's cup of tea. It's difficult to know just how to judge such things, and it's obviously important that you put your own *personal* biases well into the background, but the 'Is-this-our-kind-of-person' question *does* have to be raised on occasion. Your intuition will generally tell you when it's appropriate.

> Someone who hangs out with motorcycle gangs may not be quite this company's cup of tea.

A balanced lifestyle

Look for signs of a balanced lifestyle. *Winners*, most often, are people who both work hard and play hard. They keep things in balance. They attach importance to leisure time, and they don't waste it. They know they are most productive when they're not *always working*. They know the importance of *rewarding oneself* for one's achievements. They know that lying on a beach soaking up the sun can be productive – if one has earned it.

What does the person *do* with their leisure time? Is there evidence that they plan ahead? That they have personal goals? Do they want to learn to play the piano? Do they have a pretty clear idea of how much time they want to spend with the family every week?

Do they take good care of themselves? Do they engage in exercise and athletics? Do they consciously acknowledge the importance of being fit and healthy insofar as a productive on-the-job performer is concerned?

Summary

In this chapter we considered the fifth and final segment called Personal Life and Hobbies.

There's potentially a lot to talk about here:

- Current family situation.
- Social activities.
- Leisure time pursuits.
- Hobbies.
- General lifestyle.

- These can be time consuming. Try to zero in on meaningful matters.

The following questions from the Winner's Profile could apply to this segment:

- *Goal Orientation* seeks evidence of an activity not related to work but that includes within it some goal setting – learning to play a musical instrument or learning a foreign language.
- *Organisation* asks what planning or preparation went into setting or achieving their recreational goals.
- *Relationship-building* would look for evidence of social interaction in the candidate's hobbies.
- *Drive* looks for a competitive edge in the candidate's leisure time.
- *Stayability* asks whether there are some aspects of the candidate's leisure time that might be undesirable to the company's image.

- Look for a balanced lifestyle. Winners play hard and work hard.

CHAPTER 15

Strengths and Weaknesses

U p to now, the traditional question of *Strengths and Weaknesses* is something we have avoided putting on the agenda as a separate area for discussion. And that is because it might not be required. Through your discussion of Susan's work history, and to a lesser extent her education and career goals, you may be able to draw up a very accurate view of her strengths and weaknesses. It may not be necessary to devote a specific chunk of the interview to discussing them.

> Candidates *expect* to be asked about their strengths and weaknesses, and most will have taken time to formulate some answers.

It is also a *deceptive* area for an inexperienced interviewer, someone who doesn't interview people often enough to become really good at it, to be delving into. Candidates *expect* to be asked about their strengths and weaknesses, and most will have taken time to formulate some answers, so it is difficult to know just how much stock to put in what you hear. Is it a candid self-appraisal, or are we getting something that comes straight out of a *How-to-Win-the-Interview* book that the candidate has read?

Still, let's put it on the agenda. To do so, we should probably go back and insert it *in-between* the Work History and Career Goals segments of the first interview – the rationale being that this seems to be the spot which would allow the interview to flow most naturally.

Start with strengths

Because this area can be a bit threatening for some candidates, it's best to ask about strengths first and then shortcomings.

Try to move into the subject in a natural way that flows from the preceding 'strengths and weaknesses' label to the topic.

'*We've talked about some of the things you've achieved over the past five years, Susan... and you seem to have done quite well for yourself. What are some of the specific things about you that you feel have accounted for the success you've had?*'

Some candidates will have difficulty getting started on this question, and you might have to follow up with a gentle prod.

'*Here's the type of thing I mean. I have a daughter at home who's really inquisitive – to the point where it drives me crazy at times. But I know that's always going to be one of her real strengths and I want to encourage it.*'

If you only get one or two statements from the candidate, you can encourage them to continue simply by asking, *Is there anything else you can think of?* When prompted gently in this way, almost all candidates will be able to come up with some additional thoughts.

> Ask about strengths first and then shortcomings.

Be prepared to probe

In discussing a candidate's strengths, you should be prepared to probe a bit. Don't be too quick to accept what the candidate says as being an accurate appraisal. It might be an *honest* self-appraisal... but that doesn't mean that it is going to be an *accurate* one.

> In discussing a candidate's strengths, you should be prepared to probe a bit.

Most importantly, find out *why* something, in the candidate's view, is a strength. On what basis does he or she judge it to be a strength? Here are some example of what we mean:

- *What would you say there is about you that has accounted for your career progress to date?*
- *How exactly has that 'accounted for your career progress'...?*
- *What would you say are your main strengths? Areas where you are distinctly above-average?*
- *This probably sounds like an odd question, but... how do you know that? How do you know you're above-average in that area?*

These are powerful one-two combinations. One good question followed by another. A *Follow-up* question which puts the issue on the table and then a *Probe* which asks the candidate to go back and elaborate on his or her initial response.

With some candidates, you may wish to issue a mild challenge if you don't *agree* with their view of their own strengths and weaknesses.

'You've mentioned assertiveness as being one of your strengths. I'll be quite honest with you – it's one of the things I've been a bit concerned about...'

Why should I hire you?

It's old and it's corny, but it's still a very powerful question to ask at this stage in the interview.

'I know this sounds like a corny question, but...why should I hire you? Seriously. Give me your best sales pitch!'

Then on to weaknesses

> Weaknesses are one area where a wee bit of pressure is quite acceptable.

Then – move on to weaknesses or shortcomings. Again, do it in a natural, conversational way that flows easily.

- *How about the other side of the coin, Susan? Anything about you that you feel could be strengthened?*
- *What are the things you feel less confident about...things that you'd like to improve?*
- *What are some of the specific things you have been working on during the past year or two?*
- *With what results?*
- *How do you assess that? How do you gauge whether you've actually changed?*
- *In what specific ways do you feel you have changed or developed during the past year or two?*
- *Has that had a bearing on the results you've actually achieved in your job?*

Again, don't end this segment of the discussion too soon. This is one area where a wee bit of pressure is quite acceptable... *Anything else you can think of, John?*

Dealing with virtues-in-disguise

Most candidates realise that they are going to be asked to talk about their shortcomings at some point in the interview, and they recognise that it's not good to simply state that they don't *have* any. Most often, consciously or unconsciously, they'll start with a few innocuous items which might even be considered *virtues*. You have no doubt heard them many times.

- *I suppose my biggest weakness is that I'm too tough on myself. I expect too much from myself.*
- *I know I sometimes get impatient with people who are content to go through the motions or who expect me to do their thinking for them.*
- *I can be a bit of a maverick at times. I sometimes make people uncomfortable by coming right out and saying the unsayable.*
- *I don't suffer fools gladly. It's a bad trait, I know, and my wife gets at me about it.*
- *I'm not much of a 'policemen', I suppose. I tend to call it the way I see it, and that's got me into hot water a few times.*

This is the sort of self-congratulatory stuff you get from a relatively sophisticated candidate who's an old hand when it

> Let the person talk. Don't get your back up. Wait your turn.

comes to the interview. The person is 'confessing' to weaknesses which we *all* know are really signs of strength.

Put up with it. Let the person talk. Don't get your back up. Wait your turn. And then come back with something like:

'Well, okay, Andrew. But I can see how being too tough on people might also be considered a strength, depending on how you look at it. Is there anything that's really a shortcoming... something that you know prevents you achieving the sort of results that you would otherwise be capable of achieving?'

Let Andrew know, without being offensive or cute about it, that you can see through his ruse. Tell him quite explicitly how you define a shortcoming. Then let him talk.

A useful one-two combination

Here's a good way to get at strengths and *then* weaknesses using a single format. Ask the candidate to look ahead in time...to hypothesise:

◆ *Let's imagine you join us, and you've been here a year, and you've achieved outstanding results. What are the most likely reasons for that happening?*
◆ *Let's imagine, heaven forbid, that you've been here a year and we both decide that it's not working out. What are the most likely reasons for that happening?*

Self-Development

Your discussion with Susan about how she views her own strengths and weaknesses is an excellent time to zero in quite directly on the *Self-development* factor.

◆ *If these are your strengths, Susan, in what way have you worked to develop and fine-tune them over the years? If these are your weaknesses, what are you doing about them?*

We don't say it in those words, but that is the sense of what we talk about.

◆ *You talked about your enthusiasm as being a strength. Does that come naturally, or is it something you have to work at?*
◆ *You've said that you'd like to know more about the Marketing side of things. Have you taken any concrete steps to do that?*
◆ *You mentioned your tendency to take on too many things at one time. Is there something you've tried to do about that?*

Using a questionnaire

Asking people about their strengths and weaknesses is such an obvious thing and the candidate is almost certain to come in armed with a carefully-crafted response. It might be better to come at it from a somewhat different angle.

Here's one way to go about it.

Let's give Susan a list of 20 or so relevant strengths and ask her to earmark the five where she feels she is strongest and the five where she feels she is least strong. Then the next five strongest and the next five weakest. In effect, what we are doing is creating a frequency distribution – and what *this* does is force Susan to make choices. *This is where I'm good. This is where I'm not so good.*

Then, rather than simply asking Susan to talk about her strengths and weaknesses, we can take a copy of her questionnaire, give her a copy as well, and run through the results together.

'You indicate, Susan, that 'multi-tasking' is one of your strengths. Do you think you could expand a bit on what the term means to you?'

Summary

In this chapter we considered the traditional question of strengths and weaknesses and decided that, on balance, you could include it in your interviewing strategy if you wanted to.

- ◆ Remember, though, it can be *counter-productive* for an inexperienced interviewer because candidates expect to be asked about this and will have rehearsed answers well in advance.
- ◆ Start by asking about strengths and move into the subject in a natural way that flows from the preceding discussion without attaching a specific label to it.
- ◆ Relate the question to a specific incident either in the CV or from preceding discussions.
- ◆ Be prepared to probe.
- ◆ Ask the candidate why they think they should be offered the job.
- ◆ Move on to weaknesses or shortcomings in a smooth way, again without highlighting it.
- ◆ Don't accept self-congratulatory answers. Some candidates offer virtues in disguise.
- ◆ Get the candidates to project themselves into a successful

future in this job and ask them to list the likely reasons for that success.

◆ Link discussion here to the Self-Development theme in preceding discussions.

CHAPTER 16

Listening to What's Being Said

D uring the last several chapters, our focus has been on getting the candidate talking. We've taken pains to avoid getting into a question-and-answer session. Rather, we have tried to give the candidate – Susan – a blank slate to work with, guiding her into a subject area by issuing a broad invitation to talk. And then, resisting the temptation to jump in with specific questions, we've sat back and listened.

In this chapter, we're going to look more closely at the *listening* side of how the effective interviewer goes about his or her business.

◆ We shall examine what is involved in *Effective Listening*, and there will be some solid, practical guidelines for you to go by.

◆ We'll look at the *Reflective Response*, a good way to let the candidate *know* that you're listening, and to carry your understanding further.

◆ We'll look, finally, at the task of *dealing with silence* – and see why silence is something that should be welcomed, not kept at bay.

Effective Listening

Good listening habits form one of the essential foundation stones of the effective interview. A good interviewer knows how to listen, and knows that careful listening requires a lot of mental discipline. There is a lot to do during the interview. You have to guide the conversation, ask pertinent questions, write down whatever notes you feel are necessary, and keep an eye on the time – and these various duties can easily interfere with your concentration.

Let's look, then, at a few essential guidelines which will help ensure effective listening on your part during the interview.

- ◆ Make sure you are well prepared.
- ◆ Take steps to prevent interruptions.
- ◆ Give the candidate your full interest.
- ◆ Do things that show that you're interested.

Make sure you are well prepared

We talked about this earlier, and it is worth repeating here for emphasis. Before sitting down with the candidate, you should have done a thorough review of all the available information. You should have taken time to think through what lies ahead and develop a rough plan for the interview. And you should have taken steps to ensure that any documentation you might wish to refer to during the interview is close at hand.

Take steps to prevent interruptions

The interview cannot proceed smoothly if the telephone is ringing, or if someone is knocking on your door, or if there is a loud and very audible discussion being held in the next office.

These things obviously interfere with one's concentration, and impede both the smooth flow of conversation and the listening process. Take active steps to ensure that there will be no distractions or interruptions while the interview is taking place.

Give the candidate your full interest

This may sound very basic, but it is surprising how many people try to conduct an interview while their minds are preoccupied with other matters. It may be a specific issue that you were wrestling with that morning, or a meeting to be held later that day, or a telephone call that should have been made at least an hour ago. Regardless of where the interference is coming from, either put it out of your mind or else stop the interview and take care of it.

Do things that show that you're interested

Nod your head occasionally. Smile when the candidate says

something humorous. Use phrases such as 'That's interesting' and 'I see' to signal your interest in what's being said.

Even the occasional 'Ummm' or 'Oh-huh' or a barely audible *grunt* will do the trick. The important thing is not to sit there passively. It's not enough to listen intently. You have to *show* that you're listening intently and are interested.

The Reflective Response

The point just made is important. 'Listening' doesn't mean that we have to sit there in silence, not saying anything. A good listener doesn't just passively absorb what the other person is saying. He or she takes active steps to *encourage* that other person to talk.

The use of the *Reflective Response* is an excellent way to let the candidate know that you are really listening to what they are saying and that you are making a genuine effort to understand its meaning.

The technique is often referred to as 're-phrasing' or 're-stating', and it involves listening to what the other person is saying and then repeating it back.

Not word for word. If you just parrot back what the person

> The use of the *Reflective Response* is an excellent way to let the candidate know that you are really listening.

has said, it can't help but sound a bit artificial and mechanical. Change the words a bit. Express the thought, but use whatever words come naturally to you.

Try, in fact, to go *beyond* what the candidate has said. Try to capture the *meaning* of what was said. Try to go a wee bit beyond where the candidate left off.

Let's look at an example, and then examine why such a technique is so useful a tool.

Interview

CANDIDATE: I wasn't too happy with the way the whole thing was handled. I think Jim knew how I felt about it . . .

INTERVIEWER: But you're not sure . . . you wish now that you had spoken up while you had the chance.

CANDIDATE: Yeah . . . I probably should have said something . . .

INTERVIEWER: Why didn't you?_____

Here's another example _____

INTERVIEWER: You said earlier, Linda, that Jackie was one of the best supervisors you've ever had. What was it about her that you specially liked?

CANDIDATE: With Jackie, you knew what was expected. There was no waffling. You knew what had to be done and you knew when it had to be done by.

INTERVIEWER: You like someone who provided pretty clear direction, and Jackie was that kind of person.

CANDIDATE: Yeah. I've never really liked a boss who just says 'Well, you just go ahead and do it whatever way you feel is best...'

INTERVIEWER: Is there anything else about Jackie that you especially liked? _____

The value of the Reflective Response is that it lets the candidate know that you are making a genuine effort to understand the meaning of what they are saying. And it is a response that does not threaten the candidate or impede the flow of conversation.

You are not criticising, critiquing, or demanding that the candidate justify their statement. You are simply showing the candidate that you are interested in what is being said and that you are making a genuine attempt to understand it.

You are also giving the candidate a chance to correct you if your understanding is wrong or slightly off track. And this, in turn, is a valuable way of ensuring that you do, indeed, achieve a full and accurate understanding of what the candidate has told you.

> You are also giving the candidate a chance to correct you if your understanding is wrong or slightly off track.

Let's look at an example of how this can happen.

Interview _____

INTERVIEWER: What were the reasons for your deciding to leave the company at that stage in your career?

CANDIDATE: I wasn't really too happy with the way things were going, to be honest with you, and I really felt that a move at that stage would be the best thing for both me and the company.

INTERVIEWER: It sounds, then, like you and the company weren't getting along too well – and that leaving just seemed the best thing to do.

CANDIDATE: It's not so much that we weren't getting along. The problem was really that I had stopped growing in my job. There just wasn't anything more to look forward to, and both I and the company knew it. _____

> It's not a bad idea, at times, to deliberately *mis-state* what the candidate has told you. This is particularly helpful if you feel the candidate has avoided answering a question, or has given you only a partial or one-sided answer.
>
> In effect, you're challenging the person to come right back and correct you. And, by doing so, to go a bit further than they did the first time around.

Interview

INTERVIEWER: Given the fact that you'd had a fairly good year, Jim, why did they decide to let you go?

CANDIDATE: I wasn't really given a reason. Bob just called me into his office and gave me the news. It took five minutes. He didn't give me an explanation.

INTERVIEWER: So you have no idea why it happened. It's just one of those things which you don't understand at all.

CANDIDATE: Well, no, I wouldn't go that far. I can think of a few things that might have been involved. _____

Feelings are facts

> Among the 'facts' we're interested in are things like *emotions* and *interpretations*. This is where the Reflective Response is so useful. It helps the individual – and ourselves – pin down the emotional or cognitive events that transpired. And they are every bit as important as behavioural events.
>
> Feelings represent the candidate's *reactions* to the facts and events that have occurred. As such, they are an important source of information about the person concerned.
>
> Feelings can often be elicited by a brief, direct question. 'How did you feel about that?' or 'I guess that came as a bit of a blow, didn't it?' or 'Did that make you feel uneasy about your relationship with Mr Jackson?'

> You have to let them know, by the questions you ask, that you're interested in subjective and emotional facts as well.

It is important that you – the interviewer – take the lead in soliciting these types of reactions. Most candidates, left to their own devices, will tend to stick to the facts. So you have to let them know, by the questions you ask, that you're interested in subjective and emotional facts as well.

Dealing with silence

Most people feel uncomfortable when there is a long or noticeable pause in a conversation. There is a distinct pressure there to say something – and fill the conversational gap.

The novice interviewer is usually acutely aware of this pressure, and often jumps in quickly to repeat the question or ask a new one. The experienced interviewer is also aware of the pressure but has learned to use it to their advantage as a very valuable interviewing technique.

The candidate being interviewed, you see, is *also* feeling the pressure. And because you, the interviewer, should feel more secure in your role than the applicant, the pressure to speak is far greater for the candidate than for you.

And this is why silence is so valuable in the interview. It asks, without the use of words, 'What else can you add?' It suggests to the candidate that more is expected. It is an invitation to continue.

And the acid test of good interviewing, after all, is the *completeness* with which the candidate discusses the things that need to be discussed. If you want the candidate to give you the full story, you have to allow them enough time to do so. Once you have asked a question, assume that the candidate knows that it is their turn to speak. If a response is not immediately forthcoming, resist the temptation to jump in and repeat the question, add to it, or answer it yourself. Give the candidate a proper chance to respond.

> This is why silence is so valuable in the interview. It asks, without the use of words, 'What else can you add?'

Silence need not mean that nothing is happening. The

candidate may be thinking through what to say, or reflecting back upon past experience, or simply wrestling with a question that they have never had to answer before.

Whatever the reason, give the process a fair chance to proceed at its own pace. The information that emerges after a period of silence is often far more meaningful and relevant than that which springs from a fast-moving, non-stop discussion.

Some additional guidelines

Good interviewing is as much an art as a science. The truly effective interviewer has acquired the knack of making the whole thing seems like a relaxed, casual conversation – and yet still keeps the basic objectives in mind and gears everything toward their achievement. And there is a fair amount of 'technique' involved, regardless of how relaxed or casual things might seem on the surface.

Before we conclude this chapter, let's review a number of additional points which all pertain to the art of stimulating and maintaining a purposeful conversation. Some will be obvious, and some won't. All, though, are things which we should keep in mind as we work through the interview.

◆ Listen for the meaning of what is said.
◆ Use questions to maintain concentration.
◆ Be alert to how things are being said.
◆ Be yourself. Be as natural as you can.

Listen for the meaning of what is said

Words can be quite tricky at times, and the same word does not always mean the same thing to two different people. If the candidate uses a word or phrase which you don't quite understand – or which can obviously have more than one meaning – take time to verify your interpretation.

Ask the candidate to clarify what was meant. Or repeat back your own interpretation of what was said, and ask the candidate if that was what they intended.

Interview _____

INTERVIEWER: When you say 'deliberately', Betty, do you mean he was intentionally out to destroy the whole project?

CANDIDATE: Well, no. What I mean is that he was quite conscious of what he was doing. But I don't know that his intention was to actually destroy the project. _____

Use questions to maintain concentration

Some people find it very difficult to concentrate on what another person is saying for any great length of time. There is a limit, to be sure, to our capacity for concentration – and it will vary from one interviewer to another.

If you find your attention straying from what the candidate is saying, it may be helpful to wait for an appropriate moment and then ask a question. This is a good way of staying tuned in to the discussion.

Be alert to how things are being said

Keep a watchful eye on vocal mannerisms, inflection, gestures, facial expressions, and body posture. These are sometimes valuable clues to what the candidate is actually thinking and feeling.

Look for discrepancies between what is being said and *how* it is being said – and don't be afraid to point out your observations to the candidate. This is something that the good interviewer learns to do in a natural, positive, constructive fashion.

> Look for discrepancies between what is being said and *how* it is being said – and don't be afraid to point out your observations to the candidate.

'You've said you're excited about the job, Jacques. But I've got to be honest with you...you don't look excited.'

Then stop. Leave the discrepancy dangling in the air. The candidate will know that you expect him or her to resolve it for you. You don't have to say anything else.

Be yourself – be as natural as you can

Don't over-do eye contact. Don't over-use the various tools that we have been talking about. Don't give the candidate the impression that they are being 'techniqued'.

Be yourself. If your natural habit is to stare out of the window reflectively when someone is talking to you at length, then by all means stare out of the window. If you're in the habit of chewing on the end of a pencil, or twirling your glasses, then go ahead and do it. So long as you are listening intently to what the candidate is saying, and making a genuine and concerted effort to understand.

> Don't give the candidate the impression that he or she is being 'techniqued'.

But use common sense. If your habit is that of drumming your fingers on your desk when someone is talking to you, or glancing at your watch every few minutes, then an effort to break these habits would obviously be well advised.

Maintain a positive posture

Throughout the interview, it is important to maintain an essentially *positive* posture. The candidate should go away thinking that they have had a *good* interview, that they have made a *positive* impression. We shouldn't even mind if twelve different candidates go away thinking *they've got the job!*

> The candidate should go away thinking they have had a *good* interview.

This is important because if you think you're making a good impression, you relax. You talk more. You let things flow out of you. You become more natural.

When that begins to happen, we as interviewers begin to see the *real* person. They begin to let down their guard.

If the person hints that the main reason they were not promoted into a managerial role in their current company is that they have a boss who's been holding them back...play on it. Nod your head knowingly and say that, yeah, that's not an uncommon story...you've seen it happen all too many times before. Shake your head slowly. Why, it's a damned shame when that kind of thing happens. It's not fair.

Be a bit of an actor, is what we're saying. Adopt, consciously, an empathic, perhaps even sympathetic, perhaps even conspiratorial tone. What it does is encourage the candidate to continue. You can tell by the tone of their voice that what's coming out now is *real*.

Play down unfavourable information

When the candidate says something that is awkward or difficult to admit, it's usually something that's important – something you want to hear more about.

If you ask a direct question about the issue, or if you say *anything* in a manner that is even the least bit threatening or judgemental, you're likely to stop the free flow of information or else cause the candidate to start cautiously filtering out what they say.

Most candidates will not speak freely about a negative point or a sensitive issue once they sense that you are attaching significance to it.

So you have to play the point down. Say something that indicates that what the candidate has just told you is a common experience that happens to the best of us. If the candidate tells you that he was fired from a job because of a personality conflict with the boss, you might want to respond with something like: 'Well, there aren't too many people around who haven't had a run in with their boss at one point or another. What exactly was it that seemed to be causing the problem?'

Or, let's say that the candidate has told you that he or she failed a specific course at college and had to repeat it the next year. You might say 'Well, I never had any problems with physics when I was at school, but I bombed out in history. What was it about the physics course that you had trouble with?'

> Let the candidate know that there's nothing terribly earth-shattering about what they've admitted to.

Let the candidate know, either by what you say or the relaxed tone of your voice or by making a small confession of your own, that there's nothing terribly earth-shattering about what it is they've admitted to. In fact, you're interested. You'd like to hear more.

Avoid disagreement

Once in a while, a candidate might say something that – in normal conversation – might get your back up or bring out the debater in you.

The interview is not the time or the place for this sort of reaction. No matter what the person says, don't signal disapproval or disagreement. That is not to suggest that you have to compromise your beliefs or pretend to *approve* of something that you don't approve of. All we are saying is that you shouldn't *react*.

Say something non-judgemental that, like most of the comments you make in the interview, helps keep the conversation going. 'Well, that's an interesting comment, Jim. What makes you think that he was deliberately out to ruin the company?'

Use positive reinforcement

One of the things you can do to create an accepting, non-judgemental climate in the interview is to pay the candidate a compliment. Give them a sincere word of praise.

If the candidate tells you that he or she worked five evenings a week to help finance their education, for example, you might say: 'I like that, Judy. That's the kind of thing I'm hoping my kids will do when the time comes.'

> *Every* candidate will have something that deserves a word of praise.

It has to be sincere. Anything that smacks of insincerity or flattery or condescension will work *against* the creation of the right climate, not in favour of it. A compliment should be given in a simple, natural, straightforward fashion.

Every candidate will have something that deserves a word of praise. And there's no better way to relax a candidate, and get him or her to talk freely and spontaneously, than to give out a simple and genuine compliment when it is deserved.

Summary

In this chapter have we covered the very important skill of listening to what the candidate says during the interview and how it plays a vital part in predicting future behaviour.

We looked at some guidelines to help you with Effective Listening:

- ◆ Make sure you're well prepared.
- ◆ Take steps to prevent interruptions.
- ◆ Give the candidate your full interest.
- ◆ Do things that show you're interested.

The important gestures involved with the Reflective Response were considered:

- ◆ Take steps to encourage the candidate to talk.
- ◆ Use the technique of re-phrasing or re-stating by repeating certain key words back to the candidates, letting them know you're making an effort to understand what's being said.
- ◆ Use this technique to *go beyond* what the candidate said. Use it to encourage wider discussion.
- ◆ It is a non-threatening response.
- ◆ You are giving the candidate an opportunity to correct you if your understanding is a little off track.
- ◆ Reflective Response techniques can often elicit emotional or cognitive responses from the candidate. Responses that might not normally arise in the interview situation.

We saw how dealing with silence during the interview can be used constructively:

- ◆ The pressure to speak, instead of letting the silence continue, is much greater on the candidate than it is on the interviewer.
- ◆ It's asking the candidate what else they might have to say.
- ◆ It also gives the candidate time to think about anything they might want to add.

Some additional guidelines:

- ◆ Listen to what is being said.
- ◆ Use questions to maintain concentration.
- ◆ Be alert to how things are being said.
- ◆ Be yourself. Be as natural as you can.
- ◆ Maintain a positive posture in all you say and do during the interview. Help the candidate to relax by being supportive, then you'll see more of the real person you're interviewing.
- ◆ Play down what the candidate might think to be unfavourable information so that you can discover more about patterns of behaviour. Let the candidate know that there's nothing earth-shattering about their admission. In fact, you're interested and would like to hear more.
- ◆ Avoid disagreement. Don't say anything judgemental and always use positive reinforcement.

CHAPTER 17

Digging for Behavioural Gold

N ow we're going to get down to brass tacks. What we have covered so far are the basics. The essentials for good interviewing. We're ready now to go beyond the fundamentals.

Re-creating past performance. This is the first step, you'll recall, in our strategy for predicting the future.

What we want to do is draw up as detailed and realistic a picture of the candidate's past performance – their actual *behaviour* – as we possibly can. To re-create the past, so to speak, to the point where we can 'see' it almost as vividly as if we were actually going back through time and observing it firsthand.

And we have to do it through the candidate's own story-telling. Their description of what happened is our only link with the past.

And that link can be a very tenuous one at times. People have a way of distorting the past, recalling the good parts and forgetting the bad, reading things into other people's behaviour that simply weren't there, and putting themselves in a generally favourable light.

It's human nature, particularly when the story-teller is also the chief character in their own story. Particularly, too, when there's a job at stake and the key to getting that job, the candidate assumes, is to make sure the story is a 'good' one.

So our task is to get past the blind spots, the misinterpretations, the rationalisations, and the distortions – and get at the 'facts' of what actually happened. In much the same way that a good newspaper reporter would.

So, we've got the candidate talking. And we are working hard to pay attention and listen to what is being said. Now it's time to get down to the behavioural specifics of who said what to whom and in what tone of voice.

That's where the 'techniques' come into play. With regard

to this first and very critical task, that of re-creating the past performance, we're going to look in this chapter at what is probably the most powerful interviewing technique of all.

> Now it's time to get down to the behavioural specifics of who said what to whom and in what tone of voice.

The Behavioural Dig

We'll call our technique the *Behavioural Dig* – as opposed to an *archaeological* dig. It involves taking a specific incident or situation and delving into it deeply. Going right back into it and resurrecting what actually happened.

In the following interview candidate Robert Wentworth is talking with the interviewer, Malcolm Eadie.

Interview

MALCOLM: I'm still not sure I understand why Jack was balking at letting you go ahead with the project. The cost didn't seem to be out of line.

ROBERT: I think it was more a question of Jack's being a bit apprehensive about the fallout over in Consumer Products.

MALCOLM: How do you mean – 'fallout'?

ROBERT: We'd been getting the lion's share of the new product funding since I took over Industrial and Bill Parnell moved to Consumer, and I think Bill felt it was time to even up the score a bit.

MALCOLM: Why would that make Jack apprehensive? I'm still not sure about this word 'fallout'.

ROBERT: I think Bill had been putting some pressure on Jack to move more funding over to the Consumer side.

MALCOLM: From the way you described Jack earlier, he doesn't sound like the sort of person who would succumb to pressure from one of his underlings.

And so it goes on. Malcolm will undoubtedly continue to dig around this whole issue until he feels he understands exactly what happened and why. He suspects, most likely, that there is more here than meets the eye. Has Robert fallen out of favour with his boss? Has he been denied long-anticipated funding because his proposal just wasn't good enough? Is Bill Parnell now the rising star set to move into Jack's office when the time comes? Is that perhaps why Robert is sitting here 'exploring the marketplace'?

When to stop and dig

We obviously can't do it for everything. There just isn't time. So we have to choose carefully and dig for those answers relevant to the predictions that we are ultimately trying to make.

Here are some of the conditions under which the *Behavioural Dig* should be used:

◆ When the candidate has been reviewing their background in such broad, general terms that you haven't really been learning anything.

◆ When you sense that the candidate has been describing things in a manner designed to put themself in the most favourable light.

◆ When the incident or situation being discussed is similar to situations that the candidate would encounter if hired into the new job.

◆ When the situation is one that you yourself have had first-hand experience with, or which is simply of great interest to you.

Lead-In...Then Probe, Probe, Probe

The *structure* of a *Behavioural Dig* is fairly simple. It starts with a *Lead-in* and follows up quickly with a series of pointed *Probes* designed to create the vertical spiral that carries the discussion down to the level of behavioural specifics.

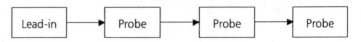

Fig. 4. The structure of a Behavioural Dig.

The *Lead-in* gives the candidate a scenario to work with, or asks them to think back to a specific type of situation that they might have encountered. Then, after letting the candidate run with the ball, we use our *Probes* to go after the details we think will be useful. It is clearly you, the interviewer, not the candidate, who is in charge of the ship.

Here are three examples:

Example 1

'As a sales rep, Lois, do you find that you sometimes have to lock horns with head office in order to get approval for something special that you want to put together for a customer? Can you give me an example?'

That's the *Lead-in*. Lois will talk for a while, but probably not in enough detail to satisfy our need to be a 'fly on the wall'. So we'll have the following *Probes* waiting in the wings:

♦ *Who was the customer?*
♦ *What was it that you were trying to do?*
♦ *I take it, then, that that sort of thing required head office approval?*
♦ *What was the reasoning behind the package you were trying to put together?*
♦ *Was there a strategy or a plan in your mind when you approached head office?*
♦ *Who did you talk to? By telephone?*
♦ *What was their initial reaction?*
♦ *How exactly did they express that to you?*
♦ *What did you do or say at that point?*
♦ *Then what happened?*

Example 2

'Let's talk for a while, Richard, about how you get along with your co-workers...the other people on the MIS team. What do you feel are some of your strengths in dealing with your co-workers?'

This is the general Lead-in question. We keep it relatively unstructured, and we let Richard tackle the subject without any further guidance. Once he begins to wind down, however, we move in with a more structured question.

'Tell me about a recent time, Richard, when you used those strengths to smooth over a situation which could easily have developed into a real argument?'

This is where we make an explicit call for Richard to take a specific situation and go into detail. To help him along, we'll have probes such as the following ready for use.

♦ *What was the problem all about?*

- *How did it get started? Who said what to whom?*
- *At what point did you sense that things were about to slide downhill?*
- *At that point, what did you say or how did you react?*
- *How did you leave things? How was the whole thing eventually resolved?*
- *Would you handle it the same way if the same situation occurred again?*

Example 3

Here's another example. The above example asked Richard to tell us about a *good* situation. Here we're asking the candidate to tell us about a situation that proved problematic or disappointing. Here's both the question and the follow-up probes:

'Tell me about the most trying time you ever had in dealing with one of your co-workers.'

- *Exactly how did the whole thing start?*
- *What did you say then?*
- *How did they respond to that?*
- *Then what happened?*
- *Anything you could have done to avoid the whole situation?*
- *Would you handle it differently, assuming you had a chance to do it over again?*

Un-questions: the prod

> When you start digging for behaviour, it may catch the candidate off-guard.

One of the advantages of digging for the behavioural specifics of what happened is that it is not something that the average candidate will be prepared for. Most candidates are anxious to make a good impression, and all but the most inexperienced will have developed certain stock answers that they've used again and again.

When you start digging for behaviour, though, it may catch the candidate off-guard. They might not quite know what it is you're getting at. Or you may find that a candidate – now that it's obvious you mean business and aren't going to be taken in by a lot of generalities and superficial descriptions – resists your efforts to probe for specifics.

Either way, we need to look here at a few special techniques for getting over the hurdle. And we want to get over the hurdle without over-relying on the *question* – remember what we said about going easy on the questions. So we use something that we'll call the 'un-question'. It comes in four different forms:

♦ The Calculated Pause.
♦ A *That's Okay* Statement.
♦ Restatement.
♦ Polite Persistence.

The Calculated Pause

It's early on in your interview with Margo Brewer, and you've just asked her to tell you what was the most challenging aspect of the customer service job which she had been in until just a couple of weeks ago. And her answer is ... total silence.

It's tempting to jump in and say something, just to break the silence – rephrase the question, or expand upon it, or skip it altogether and move onto something else.

The best advice is not to rush. Use what might best be called a *Calculated Pause*. Just sit there a bit and wait – ten seconds or so ought to do it. Ten seconds doesn't sound like a long time – but in an interview it can seem like an eternity.

Your silence puts the pressure on the candidate to say something. It makes it clear that it's their turn to speak, not yours.

It might be that Margo just needs a little time to gather her thoughts or to sort out what's important and what's not. Remember: the sort of interviewing we're doing is aimed at getting the candidate to *think*. So we need to give him or her plenty of time to do that. Don't rush.

A *That's Okay* Statement

Margo still hasn't said anything, and the silence has gone on now for a good 15 seconds. What started as a *Calculated Pause* is fast becoming an *awkward* pause. What do we do now?

Don't panic. Let's break the silence. But let's do it without letting Margo off the hook and skipping on to the next question. Instead, use what might best be thought of as a That's Okay statement.

'I know it's sometimes a bit difficult to think back and remember precisely what happened. When I ask people a question like that, if often takes them a moment or two – but that's okay because I learn a lot when we look at exactly what happened.'

What the That's Okay Statement does is tell the candidate that it's okay not to have a quick answer. It happens to most people. Relax, don't worry about it. Don't get self-conscious.

This is important, because the last thing in the world you want to see happen is for the candidate to become nervous and self-conscious. To talk freely and explore things spontaneously, you have to be relaxed.

By the way, make sure you smile sympathetically when you issue a That's Okay Statement. Your words and your manner have to be 'in synch'. If you frown or glance at your watch or let a tone of irritation creep into your voice, nothing you can say will prevent the candidate from tightening up even more.

Restatement

Margo *still* hasn't said anything. By now it's quite clear that she hasn't been using the silence to think things through or sort her ideas out. She's frozen up. She's at a loss for words. And something more than a That's Okay Statement is going to be needed to unfreeze her.

Our next technique is a simple restatement of the question. Don't repeat it word for word. If you do that, you're *bound* to let a hint of impatience creep into your voice – because that's what people do when they're impatient: they repeat what they've just said word for word.

Change the wording slightly. Shift the emphasis a bit.

'What I'm looking for, Margo, is an example from your job at United of something that really put you to the test – a problem or a situation that was a real challenge for you... Can you recall something like that?'

Polite Persistence

Clive, a candidate for an important supervisory role in our corporate accounting area, has stated quite proudly that one of his real strengths is that he isn't afraid to challenge the status quo and be something of a maverick. And that's good, because one of the things you want the new supervisor to do is be *innovative*. And being innovative is going to require that the person not be afraid to be a bit of a rebel and challenge some long-standing practices and assumptions.

Still, we need to see some evidence. We aren't going to just take Clive's assessment of himself at face value.

'Can you think of a specific example of your doing that, Clive – challenging the status quo, I mean? A specific example from the past couple of months?'

And he says:

'Well, it's something I do a lot of. It's just part of the way I approach things. If it means challenging the status quo, I'm not afraid to do it.'

Here, the candidate seems to be trying to dodge the question, and your task is to point out as tactfully and as politely as you can that evasion just isn't going to work. If you let the candidate get the better of you, you'll have set the tone for the rest of the interview, and it will be a downhill slide from here on in.

So we have to stand firm. *Polite Persistence* is the order of the day.

'I realise it's a bit difficult to come up with specific examples, Clive, but can you think of a recent situation where you "challenged the status quo"?'

Questions and answers

Generalities versus specifics

Why so much emphasis on picking apart specific incidents? Isn't it better to talk about the person's skills in general? After all, isn't that what we're hiring?

If you ask someone a general question – '*How do you go about organising projects?*' – you're likely to get a pretty general answer. '*I tend to do this. I try to do that. I try not to do this. I keep an eye open for that.*'

Then you're left with the question: *Can I trust what they're telling me?* How do I know if it's true? Even if they aren't consciously pulling the wool over my eyes, maybe they don't *know* how they organise projects? Maybe they're just saying what seems logical, or what they think they're *supposed* to say. Or maybe they're telling me what they *try* to do but three times out of five it doesn't work and they end up scrambling.

After all, how many people are going to come right out and tell you that no, I'm *not* very well organised. I'm *terrible* at organising projects. And yet we *know* that not everyone's good at it.

It's better – much better – to ask the person to tell you how they organised the *ABC* project, or the *XZY* project. How did you go about organising *that specific project?*

One reason why this is good is that no one has ever asked them how they organised that specific project. So you're not going to get a prepared answer.

That leads to reason number two. Because they haven't had to think about this before, they're going to have to think about it now. They're going to have to *think*. You'll be able to watch them as they actually think through a problem. It's a glorious opportunity to actually see them in action, first-hand.

And the third reason is that it comes closest to what we agreed the ideal was – the ideal being to be a fly on the wall and actually watch a person perform in their current job for one whole day. If we could do that, we wouldn't be watching how they organise projects *in general*. We would watch them as they organise a *specific* project.

And when we hire them, we aren't going to hire them to organise projects *in general*. We're going to hire them to organise the *DEF* project and the *HIJ* project.

Behaviour versus outcomes

Rather than putting so much emphasis on finding out about the candidate's past *behaviour*, shouldn't we focus on the *results* that they have achieved...and judge them on that basis?

The main reason for digging for behaviour is because behaviour is where we see the *patterns* that tell us what kind of person the candidate is. And it's by understanding what kind of person the candidate is that we are able to predict the future.

Let's clarify some terms here:

◆ *Behaviour:* This is what actually happens. Jim says this. Judy does that. Bill reacts this way. Harry handles the meeting that way.

◆ *Outcomes:* These are the results of that behaviour. Sales increased. Three people got up and left. Candidate got promoted.

◆ *Environment:* And all this took place in a particular environment. *B* produced *O* under this or that set of conditions.

We see a lot of the *O* information on the CV. The *Outcomes*. And we'll hear a lot of it during the interview.

The person tells us that he or she opened twelve new accounts over a two-year period, or increased sales by 23% in the first year, or was named to the President's Club three years in a row.

Can they come in and do the same sort of thing for us? *That's* the real question.

We're intelligent enough to tread carefully here, knowing that the *E* factor is important... the environment here isn't the same as the environment there. We're not so naive as to assume that we can do a direct, one-to-one extrapolation.

But what we don't do enough of is go *backward* from the outcomes and look at the *behaviour* that produced that outcomes.

How did they manage to open twelve new accounts over that two-year period? If we take any *one* of those accounts, how exactly did they land *that* particular account? If landing that account hinged on two or three crucial meetings with the prospective customer, let's take *one* of those meetings and ask ourselves how the individual handled that specific meeting? *Within* that meeting, how did they handle this-or-that particular objection, or this-or-that particular point?

And so on.

Why do we do this? Because we're not hiring the Outcomes We're not hiring the Environment. We're just hiring the individual... All we're really going to get is the individual's *Behaviour.*

So what we have to do is predict what sort of Behaviour we're going to be getting. And what Outcomes that behaviour is likely to produce... in *our* unique Environment.

When we look at it this way, it reinforces the idea that the concept of *Personality* is nothing more than a shorthand way of describing certain *patterns* of behaviour – certain tendencies or habits or *ways* of behaving – that the person will be bringing into the new job in the new environment.

It's those *patterns* that we're really hiring, of course, not the actual behaviour – that's gone, over and done with, past tense. But if we don't see the behaviour, we won't see the patterns.

We'll know what Outcomes the person was able to produce in this or that previous Environment... but we won't be in a position to do what we're supposed to be doing – and that's predicting the future.

Summary

In this chapter we saw how the interview process became more specific with the interviewer digging for more information. Digging for *behavioural specifics.*

- ◆ The *Behavioural Dig* helps us to re-create past performance in the interview situation. It gets us nearer to the real facts of what has happened. It involves us taking a particular event and delving into it until a genuine understanding has been achieved.

- ◆ It involves probing to re-create what actually happened.

Some candidates might not be prepared for your deeper, probing, questions:

- ◆ Use the Calculated Pause.
- ◆ Use a *That's Okay* Statement.
- ◆ Use the Restatement technique.
- ◆ Use Polite Persistence.

◆ Remember that candidates can distort the past, recalling good parts and brushing over the bad.

◆ This allows you to *observe* the candidate *at work*. You'll see how they think through a problem, respond to events or deal with people in a sensitive situation.

◆ You get a *feel* for the candidate's abilities and possible strategies.

◆ Use questions and answers thoroughly. Don't settle for general answers. Go for specifics.

◆ Make the candidate address a problem. Watch their behaviour as they work through it. Make them *think*.

We also looked at behaviour versus outcomes:

◆ Behaviour is what really happens.

◆ Outcomes are the results of that behaviour.

◆ We must also include *environment* here as it affects behaviour and outcomes. *B* produced *O* under this set of conditions.

◆ Remember that environment is all-important. It affects patterns of behaviour.

◆ Ask the candidate exactly how they created the environment for the success they claim to have achieved. Keep digging until you're satisfied with the answer.

CHAPTER 18

Probing for Specific Competencies

In this chapter we are going to tailor our questioning to what we know about the specific demands of the job for which the candidate is being considered. For example:

◆ Internal Consulting Skills
◆ Project Management
◆ Attention to Detail
◆ Customer Relationships
◆ Management Style
◆ People Development.

We'll use the *Behavioural Dig* – our potent combination of a scenario-setting *Lead-in* followed by a series of sharp *Probes* – to get the candidate to reach back into his or her work experience and resurrect an example of a specific competency in action. A total situation, one in which the competency was highlighted – *Talk to me, Susan, about a situation where you had to exercise leadership.*

Some general points.

◆ Obviously, we're probing for behavioural specifics. The more we get at actual behaviour, the more we learn about how the candidate actually performs.

◆ Our questions start out being quite broad and unstructured as we lead the candidate into the area. Then we begin to narrow them down and make them more structured.

◆ We try to probe for positive things first. We do not want this to be a cross-examination or an inquisition. Then we shift our focus to the less complimentary side of the ledger.

◆ We won't always ask the same questions in the same order. We *still* – even here – want the conversation to flow as naturally as possible. We have to 'go with the flow'.

◆ Some of the questions might not even have to be asked at all if the information we are after is volunteered. The questions are just tools to be used when and if we need them.

Internal consulting skills

'I know an important part of your job is the quality of the relationships you are able to establish and maintain with end-users. What are some of your strengths in this area?'

That's the general Lead-in. It guides the candidate into the area we want to talk about. Once he or she has talked a bit, usually in relatively general terms, we get down to specifics:

'Sometimes a client – a user – comes to us for help and isn't quite sure what they want. Can you think of an example of this happening to you?'

- *What was the situation?*
- *How did the client approach you? What did they say?*
- *What did you say then?*
- *Is this how you would normally handle that type of situation?*
- *Can you think of another example?*

In the above example, we're looking for how a systems person helps an end-user define his or her needs. It's a very important part of what makes an internal consultant successful.

'Tell me about the most frustrating experience you've had, trying to help a client or end-user solve a problem.'

- *What exactly was the situation?*
- *How did the client present the problem to you initially?*
- *How exactly did they say that?*
- *How did you respond?*
- *Then what happened?*
- *What was it about the situation that made it so frustrating for you?*
- *What happened in the end?*

'I am sure there are times when you have to deal with an irate customer or end-user. Can you think of a time when you really felt good about how you handled an awkward situation?'

- *What exactly was the problem?*
- *How was it brought to your attention?*
- *How did they say that? Was it said in an angry voice?*
- *Putting yourself in their shoes, do you think their anger was justified?*
- *How did you approach things from that point on?*
- *Exactly how did you say that?*
- *Strategically, do you feel now that that was the right way to handle it?*
- *How was the situation resolved?*

Amongst other things, we're looking for empathy here – the ability to put oneself in the shoes of the other person and to see things through their eyes. We're also looking for strategic insight and sensitivity in terms of how the candidate then dealt with the problem at hand.

'I know it's sometimes difficult to get a complex idea – something technical – across to a user or client who lacks technical knowledge. Can you tell me about a time when you felt you did that sort of thing quite successfully?

- *What exactly was the situation?*
- *What was the concept that you were trying to get across?*
- *How exactly did you do it? Act it out a bit – pretend I'm the client...*
- *What did the client say?*
- *How did you know you had got the point across successfully?*

Note the use of a mini-roleplay here. *Act it out a bit – pretend I'm the client.* There's no better way to let the candidate know that you really and quite literally want to go back in time and 're-create past performance'.

Project management

We're interviewing June Richardson, and the job at stake is that of systems analyst. It's a busy front-line job with the very practical objective of keeping the computers up and running, developing special software applications, keeping the company abreast of new technology, and doing a lot of general-purpose trouble-shooting.

One of the things that's going to be absolutely critical to successful performance in the job is the ability to manage a heavy workload.

It's not just going to be a *heavy* workload, it's going to be a multi-faceted, constantly-shifting, back-and-forth kind of heavy workload. Lots of different priorities, multiple demands on one's time, lots of different people to keep happy.

The person is going to have to be able to keep six or seven balls in the air at one time. They need to be able to maintain a difficult balance between important long-term projects and immediate and unanticipated crises that require instant attention. There'll be pressure coming from all sides – deadlines that have to be met, fires that have to be put out, clients that have unrealistic expectations about what can and can't be achieved, and so on.

The candidate's ability to pull off this sort of juggling act is one of those things that we have to assess. It's an important topic about which we have to generate hypotheses and look for evidence to translate those hypotheses into solid predictions.

The important thing is this. We can't leave it to chance. We have to force the issue. We have to put it on the agenda. It's early in the interview. We've used a broad-brush question to get June talking about the work she has been doing during the past several years. To this point, though, she hasn't talked specifically about how she organises projects or deals with multiple demands on her time – which is the area we want to delve into. So we use a *Follow-up*.

'I'd like to talk a bit now about how you organise and manage your projects. Could you tell me a little bit about how you do it?'

That's about as specific as we should be. If we get any more specific – if we ask June how she responds to an urgent and unexpected request, for example, or what approach she takes to keeping six or seven different projects up in the air at one time – we'll end up telegraphing what we're after.

So we keep the *Follow-up* fairly general. And then we let June talk.

At some point, June will begin to wind down her discussion, and there may be some key points that she has not yet covered. We can see that she has good planning and organising skills... and that's reassuring. But can she operate effectively in a fast-moving environment where urgent demands are being thrown at her from all sides? We need to find out. So we use a *Follow-up* to the *Follow-up*. A bit narrower in scope this time. A bit more explicit.

'I know in my job, June, I have a lot of different clients that I have to keep happy – and everyone seems to want their project done "yesterday". Can you think back to a time when you had a lot of programmes that had to be written and very little time to do them?'

Notice what we're doing here. We're asking June to think back to one specific time, one actual period of time, when she had lots to do and not a lot of time to do it. That's a sort of pressure we know is going to be involved in the job, and we want to get a feel for how she performs in that type of situation.

Then come the *Probes*, our powerful tool for fleshing out the behavioural specifics. Remember, our aim is to go back in time and re-create past performance. To be a 'fly on the wall'.

♦ *When did this take place?*
♦ *How did you go about allocating your time across the different projects that had to be completed?*
♦ *Did you have to put in any overtime to get everything done?*
♦ *Were you eventually able to get all the programs written? How did you manage it?*
♦ *How often does this sort of log-jam occur, over an average six-month period, let's say?*

> Remember, our aim is to go back in time and re-create past performance. To be a 'fly on the wall'.

'When did this take place?' is a useful question to ask. June might have started off by saying 'Well, I can recall one time when...'. Asking her to pin it down – Was it last week? Last month? Halfway through September? – sets the tone. It helps June *focus*. It underscores the fact that we are probing for specifics.

Follow-up... and then *Probe, Probe, Probe*. That's the

'technique'. That's how we dig for behaviour. Here's another example:

'Can you think of a specific project – during the past three months, let's say – where you really felt good about being able to bring it to completion on time (or within budget)?'

Again, as she answers this question, we bring in increasingly structured questions to help us probe for the specifics:

♦ *What were the deadlines you were working under? How were they originally set?*
♦ *Were they realistic?*
♦ *What were the obstacles you were facing that threatened to push the project off-target?*
♦ *How did you deal with them?*
♦ *How did you go about deciding to handle them in that fashion? What was the reasoning?*
♦ *Did you have to get any unusual help or support from anyone else?*

Let's look at one more example of this powerful one-two combination – *Follow-up* question and then the *Probes* – in action. We're still with June. Having asked her to tell us about a specific project that she felt *good* about, we ask her now to talk about a specific time when things did *not* run so smoothly:

'See that file over there? It was supposed to be out of this office three days ago, and into the hands of an eagerly-waiting client. I'm sure that sort of thing happens to you from time to time. Tell me about one of your projects that fell seriously behind schedule.'

We've eased her into this area by making a small confession of our own. We've been known to get behind on projects, too. It's human. In effect, we're telling June that we won't hold it against her if it turns out that she has had a similar experience. Here are some of the *Probes* we can use to help us dig for specifics:

♦ *What was the project? Who was it for?*
♦ *What were the obstacles you ran into?*
♦ *What did you do to try to overcome them?*
♦ *What were the consequences of the delay for the client who had asked for the work?*

+ *Were you able to take any steps to prevent that sort of delay from happening again?*
+ *During all of last year, what percentage of your projects fell behind schedule?*

Attention to detail

There are many roles in which a careful attention to detail is critical to successful performance. Buyers, analysts, chemists, accountants, people in the inventory control section – these are all people who can't afford to be casual or cavalier in the way they handle detail. Their observations and measurements, their checking of what goes through their area, has to be spot on. So it's something we put on the agenda:

'*I know that catching errors is an important part of your job. Can you think back to the error you caught during the past year that saved your company the most money?*'

That's the general *Follow-up* question that we use to direct the candidate into this area. Then come the *Probes*:

+ *When did that happen?*
+ *What exactly was the mistake or error?*
+ *Who made it?*
+ *Was it just a case of carelessness, do you think, or was it something else?*
+ *How did you catch it?*
+ *What did you do then?*
+ *Did you take any steps to discourage that type of error in the future?*

Notice that we asked the candidate to *think* a bit about what *caused* the mistake or error that she was able to catch. Was it just a case of carelessness, or something else? What a person *thinks*, either now or at the time when the incident happened, is every bit as *behavioural* as what they did or what events transpired. So when you're probing for specifics, don't overlook *cognitive* specifics.

'*What went through your mind when you saw that? Do you think he really meant it? How did you interpret that? Why do you think she decided not to go along with the idea?*

Here's another *Follow-up*, designed to tell us what happens when an error or mistake, despite the candidate's best efforts, *does* get through:

'I guess no matter how hard we try, there are always going to be a few errors that slip by unnoticed... What's the worst one you can think of – during the past year, let's say?'

♦ *What exactly was the mistake or error that you let slip by?*
♦ *How often would that sort of mistake normally occur, would you think?*
♦ *How did it finally come to your attention?*
♦ *What did you say?*
♦ *Have you taken any steps to guard against that sort of thing happening again?*

This last probe is important. What has the person learned? What specific steps, if any, have they taken to prevent a repeat of the situation being described?

Next, we have a two-part question. A general, conversational Lead-in followed by the much more structured request that we look in detail at one specific example.

'I know when I'm in a hurry I sometimes rush things a bit and don't give them as much care or attention as I'd like. As a result, I end up having to do the whole job over again. Does that sort of thing ever happen to you? Can you think of a specific example from the past month or so? I'd like to know how you handled it.'

♦ *What exactly was the job or the task?*
♦ *Were you under special time pressures?*
♦ *In what way did you 'rush it through' or not take enough care?*
♦ *Did you actually have to do the whole job over again?*
♦ *Has the same sort of situation presented itself again?*

One last example:

'Could we talk in some detail about how you prepared for that meeting, Janis...'

♦ *How far in advance of the meeting did you start preparing?*
♦ *What specific things did you do?*

- *How much time did you spend on that?*
- *Did you consult with anyone from outside the company?*
- *How much of that was written down?*

Here, we're simply observing how much attention to detail was displayed in the candidate preparing for a specific meeting. Preparing for a presentation, putting together a report or a proposal, doing a project... these are good places to assess just how much attention the person gives to the fine details.

> Preparing for a presentation, putting together a report or a proposal, doing a project... these are good places to assess just how much attention the person gives to the fine details.

Customer relationships

'I suppose an important part of your job, Ruth, involves dealing with the public. What would you say your strengths are when it comes to dealing with people?'

That's the *Lead-in*. Using a relatively unstructured question, we ask Ruth to talk about one specific aspect of her work – her strengths in the area of dealing with the public.

A bit later, we narrow the focus down with a much more structured question and some digging. Here's both the question and the subsequent *Probes*.

'Can you think back to the last time when you really went out of your way to do something extra for a customer?'

- *What exactly was the situation?*
- *What did you do or say to help the person?*
- *How did the person respond?*
- *How often does this type of thing happen in, let's say, a six-month period?*
- *Can you think of another example?*

Having asked the candidate about a *positive* example of dealing with the public, we can now look at the other side of the ledger:

'I'm sure there are times when having to deal with a customer can be a real chore. Tell me about a time that was especially frustrating or difficult for you?'

- ◆ *When exactly did this happen?*
- ◆ *What was it about the situation that made it so frustrating?*
- ◆ *How did you react?*
- ◆ *How did the customer respond to that?*
- ◆ *Then what happened?*
- ◆ *How was the situation resolved?*
- ◆ *Has it coloured the relationship you have today with the customer?*
- ◆ *How often would you say that this sort of thing happens?*

Here's another combination of a structured question and *Probes*:

'I'm sure there are times when you've had to say "no" to a customer . . . when they wanted something they couldn't have, or wanted you to do something you couldn't do. Can you think back to a specific example?'

- ◆ *When did this happen?*
- ◆ *What was it, exactly, that the customer was after?*
- ◆ *Why couldn't you go along with that?*
- ◆ *How did you explain?*
- ◆ *What did the customer say?*
- ◆ *Then what did you say?*
- ◆ *How was it left?*

Management style

'Tell me a little bit about your management style, Susan.'

People usually know what 'management style' refers to, so this brief *Follow-up* is really all that's needed to get the candidate talking.

'When you say "supportive", Susan, what exactly do you mean by that? "Supportive" in what sense?'

When people use terms such as *supportive* or *hands-off*, or when they talk about such things as giving people lots of *autonomy*, it's best to check exactly what interpretation they are applying to these commonly used labels. Start by asking for a simple elaboration. Then press for some specifics:

'Can you give me an example, Richard, of your management of someone in a "firm but fair" manner? A specific incident?

- *What exactly was the situation?*
- *When did it happen?*
- *How did you say that to him (her)?*
- *How did he (she) respond?*
- *What happened after that?*

'Can you think of a specific situation where your management style "backfired" or wasn't quite what was needed to get the results you were after?'

- *What exactly was happening in the situation?*
- *When was this?*
- *What was your initial approach to handling it?*
- *What response did you get?*
- *What happened then?*
- *How would you handle that same situation if it happened today?*

'Are there situations in which your management style has to be adjusted, Frank? I'm thinking of such things as month-end, when everything has to be done in a hurry, or crisis situations, or particular types of problems?'

We're still on the subject of management style but now we're narrowing it down a bit further to the issue of *adjusting* one's management style to suit the situation at hand. Let the candidate give you a general answer. Then narrow it down again and press for a specific example:

'Can you think back to a specific example of that happening?'

- *What exactly was the situation?*
- *When was this?*
- *In what way did your normal style of managing have to be adjusted?*
- *What was there about the situation that you felt called for that approach?*
- *What eventually happened?*

We're looking here for signs of intelligent flexibility. There are times when even a supportive manager has to bark out orders or take charge of things, or when the normally hands-off executive has to roll his or her sleeves up and get directly involved in things.

'*When you moved into the Controller's position, Judy, did your management style change in any specific way?*'

♦ *When you say more 'hands-off', what exactly do you mean by that?*
♦ *Can you give me a specific example?*
♦ *Was it a conscious change? Something you sat down and thought about?*

People development

This is an important area to delve into when we're interviewing candidates for a managerial position. How much time does the candidate spend on the development of subordinates? What approach is taken? How much emphasis is there on working with people on a day-to-day basis as opposed to relying exclusively on the year-end appraisal?

'*Let's talk for a while, Roger, about the role you have played in developing the people under you. I think you mentioned in your covering letter that you viewed yourself as a good developer of people...*'

This is our general Lead-in question. We're inviting Roger to talk generally about the subject of people development. A bit later, we can come back with more structured Follow-up questions and then Probe for specifics.

'*During the past year-and-a-half, Roger, is there one subordinate in particular that you really feel was able to blossom as a result of the efforts you made as manager?*'

Again – the obvious thing. We ask Roger to zero in on one specific person. And we start with a 'success story'. Here are some of the *Probes* that might come in handy:

♦ *Who exactly was this person?*
♦ *What was their job?*

- *What were the areas in which you felt they needed development?*
- *How did you work on that area? Why? What was your strategy?*
- *Tell me in more detail just how you discussed it with the person.*

Probe for specifics. If Roger tells you that he had a long discussion with the subordinate, find out what they talked about. In detail. What exactly did Roger say? How did the subordinate respond to that? What did Roger say then?

'Can you think back to a time, Roger, when you really put a lot of time into working with one of your people – and the person just didn't seem to respond?'

- *Who exactly was the person?*
- *What was it, specifically, that you were trying to work on?*
- *What approach did you take?*
- *How did the person respond?*
- *Would you handle it differently if you could go back and do it over again?*

Now – a *general* question. You and Roger have talked about the development of people. Now let's ask him to *summarise* what he feels are the real keys to successful people development:

'In your experience, Roger, what's the real key to developing people? What is it that really makes the difference?'

And now, if you want, you can follow-up with yet another round of digging:

'Can you think of a specific example of where you put those principles into action?'

- *Who was the person you were trying to work with?*
- *What were the areas that you felt that they had to work on?*
- *What approach did you take?*
- *How did they respond?*

Summary

In this chapter we have tailored our questions to the specific demands of the job. We also looked at how to use the Behavioural Dig technique to seek the following competencies not always found on the Winner's Profile.

Internal consulting skills:

- ◆ The quality of the relationships with end-users. Get into the specifics of certain situations.
- ◆ Look for empathy, strategic insights and sensitivity.
- ◆ How would the candidate manage such a situation?
- ◆ Use case studies or mini role-play to help re-create past performance.

Project management:

- ◆ Can the candidate cope with a heavy workload?
- ◆ Can the candidate maintain a constantly changing set of priorities? What evidence is there of this?

Attention to detail:

- ◆ Ask the candidate for specific details of an event already covered in discussion or that is in their CV.
- ◆ Link this to tasks in the job on offer to help in establishing patterns of behaviour.

Customer relationships:

- ◆ Look for specific examples of how the candidate deals with people. Keep digging. Use mini role-play if necessary.
- ◆ Ask the candidate about a positive and a negative example of dealing with the public.

Management style:

- ◆ Because most candidates know what this means go straight into more probing questioning.
- ◆ Check that you all know what is meant by phrases like 'hands off' support or 'autonomy'.
- ◆ Ask for specific examples of management style and how it would apply in our company.

People development:

- ◆ How important is the development of subordinates? How would they organise it in our company?

- ◆ Which is best – day-to-day support and development or end-of-year appraisal?

- ◆ Again, use a specific example and keep digging. Use mini role-play within our company if it helps.

CHAPTER 19

Pattern-Spotting

A n ordinary conversation generally proceeds on one level. Two people sit together and talk about 'things'. Such things might include recent happenings at the office, the upcoming Formula One race or football match or a recent national disaster.

An interview, on the other hand, is something more than just a conversation. It is a conversation-with-a-purpose. And the purpose is that of deciding whether candidate X has what it takes to do job Y. To be precise, our task is to look for the patterns in the candidate's past behaviour and compare these with the requirements of the job. With this purpose in mind, we have to conduct the selection interview on *two* levels.

Spotting potential

The first is the *factual* level. We need to carry on a discussion about the candidate's background, current situation, and outlook on the future. We need to discuss *facts* – be they past events, experiences, decisions, thoughts, feelings, ideas, actions, or reactions.

The second is the *inferential* level. Discussing the facts is not enough. Our more important task is to look for the behavioural patterns which they contain – and use these to predict on-the-job performance. We need, in short, to translate facts into *hypotheses*.

We notice, for example, that candidate Tom Patchett expresses his ideas using a lot of clichés that don't quite fit. We notice, too, that he doesn't always seem to grasp the subtleties in the questions we ask – he takes them literally. He also acknowledges that he prefers dealing with tangible, here-and-now problems that have a right-or-wrong *solution* rather than wrestling with sticky 'issues'. His discussion of technical and factual matters, during the interview, is lucid and well organised but when the talk turns to broader issues, such as where the industry as a whole is going, he seems to stumble.

These are the facts. This is what we've noticed about Tom in the interview. And then we start to draw up hypotheses:

- *Not a conceptualiser.*
- *Oversimplifies.*
- *Better in a technical analytical role.*
- *Management potential?*

> One important task is to predict on-job performance from behavioural patterns.

Note that we've gone from gathering information about what the candidates *does* or *did* to generating hypotheses about what sort of *person* he or she is. We've moved from the specific to the general. From the level of behaviour to the level of behavioural *pattern* – or 'personality'.

And it is this movement, this mental shift, that gets to the very heart of what an effective interview is all about.

The factual level

This is where most people spend most of their time when they're conducting an interview.

It's the factual level. You're sitting there talking with the candidate about the basic facts of their background – who they are, where they've been in their career, what they've managed to accomplish along the way, why they're interested in exploring a move at this stage in the game.

Even at this level, of course, there's all sorts of room for the average interviewer to fine-tune their skills and improve their performance. If all you ever did, in fact, was to follow the advice that we've set out so far, the chances are good that you'd come away a better interviewer.

Our main message has been that you shouldn't just be 'gathering' surface facts at this level. You should be digging for actual behaviour. Probing. Cutting through the questionable self-descriptions and meaningless generalities that fill up the average interviewing session. Putting some real flesh on the skeletal facts that are there in the candidate's CV or application form.

You've got to *re-create* the candidate's past behaviour and past performance – right there in the interviewing room. Go back and actually observe him or her in action, so to speak. Get a feel for how they actually behaved, what actually happened, what exactly was said by whom and in what tone of voice.

But there's more. We've already taken a major step toward more effective interviewing, but we're still a long way from the finishing line. There's a whole other level of interviewing, and it's here that the truly professional interviewer spends the bulk of his or her time.

The inferential level

Interviewing somebody is a little bit like watching a football match. The average interviewer never even sees the match. All they get is the candidate's watered-down version of it. It's like a scouting report – except that it's usually marred by a generous sprinkling of perceptual distortions and emotional stress.

The good interviewer gets to see the match. He or she probes for detail, digs for behavioural facts, fleshes out the specifics – until he or she can almost 'see' the action unfolding right before their very eyes.

The *really* effective interviewer goes a step further.

The skilful interviewer doesn't just watch the match – they analyse it. Like a shrewd manager or coach trying to get a bead on next Saturday's opponent. Trying to detect the strategies that are at work, searching for weak spots and predictable patterns that can be pounced on or exploited in the up-coming match.

They watch the match, but they're not totally absorbed by it. They're not leaning forward in their seat, alternately clenching their fist and letting out great whoops of joy as their side struggles toward a hard-won victory or disappointing loss.

No, they're cool. Detached. Discerning. Analytical. Glancing down to their notepad from time to time, and jotting down little reminders that they want to think about long after the game is over. In fact, they're not even all that concerned about who wins or loses – they're just there to take a look at next Saturday's opponent in action. They're there to see what makes the team tick.

And that's how an effective interviewer operates. They are skilled at creating action – on the *factual* level – but that's really nothing more than a means to an end. What they are really after are clues as to what sort of person they are dealing with. The re-created action is just the data that they have to work with.

Looking for the patterns

We introduced the word 'personality' to refer to the patterns that show up in a person's behaviour across time and from one situation to another. Once we've gone back and re-created the person's past performance, our next task is to look very

> The common threads represent that individual's 'person-ality' at work, and they are the key to predicting what sort of performance can be expected in the future.

carefully at that performance and see if we can't discover some basic patterns or common threads running through it.

The common threads represent that individual's 'personality' at work, and they are the key to predicting what sort of performance can be expected in the future.

Finding words to describe them

Finding words to describe these common threads is a crucial task. The challenge here is to move from observing that the candidate *did* such-and-such a thing to saying that they are such-and-such a type of person.

Thus, for example, we might end up saying that Joe is a 'hard-driving manager' or that Judy is a 'stickler for detail' or that Mary 'doesn't suffer fools gladly'. It is not necessary that we get into such fancy areas as 'ego strength' and 'need for autonomy'. What counts is that we understand how the person operates.

Facts and hypotheses

There's probably one single error that inexperienced interviewers make more than any other, and that's to gather up a lot of 'facts' about the candidate's past and yet come away from the interview with little or no idea of what sort of *person* they've been talking to.

We can start to correct that situation right now, by looking for patterns in the candidate's past behaviour or performance, and then translating what we find into personality-type terms of the sort alluded to above.

Here are some guidelines that might prove helpful:

◆ Keep your eyes open for possible patterns.
◆ Keep track of your hypotheses.
◆ Look for confirming evidence.
◆ Build a catalogue of models.

Keep your eyes open for possible patterns

Watch for them. That's all that's involved here. Don't let yourself get too involved in the conversation. Keep part of your mind free to spot the patterns that are there in the candidate's description of what happened. Even while you're talking with the candidate about the details of this or that particular situation, your mind should be actively searching for patterns and common threads in what is being said.

It's like being a detective. If you walk into a room, and you're looking for clues, then you'll probably end up finding them. If you're not a detective, and you're not looking for clues, then you're quite likely to walk into that very same room and not see a thing.

Too many interviewers get carried away with the 'interviewing' portion of their job, almost as if they were hosting a talk show or digging up material for a newspaper article. They forget that they're supposed to be detectives as well.

Keep track of your hypotheses

And that's what they'll be at this stage of the game. Hypotheses.

- Stamina?
- Long-terms goals uncertain.
- Hands-off manager.
- Too aggressive?

Jot these things down on the paper you're using to take notes. If need be, divide the notepad in half and use the lefthand side to record the *facts* of the candidate's background and the righthand side to record your hypotheses as they come to you.

Think you see a pattern there? Find a brief word or two to describe it, and then jot it down.

Look for confirming evidence

When you think you've spotted a pattern in the candidate's past behaviour or performance, treat it as a *hypothesis* until you've seen the pattern showing through again at some other time or in some other context. Then, when you've seen it again, go back to your original note and put a tick beside it.

You'll probably spot at least two or three major patterns in each candidate's behaviour, and you'll know they're the major ones because they'll end up with three or four ticks beside them.

Do you see consistent signs that the person takes people at face value – and sometimes get burned in the process? Or tackles problems very methodically and cautiously, even in situations where quick and expedient action is what's called for? Or works best in companies that are small and relatively free of red tape?

These are the sorts of patterns you're looking for. They're the very stuff of what we mean when we talk about 'personality'.

Build a catalogue of models

An audience of novice interviewers was once told:

'There are two types of people in the world. Those who look at a forest and see a bunch of trees and those who look at a bunch of

trees and see a forest. I want you to listen to a series of five-minute extracts, taken from actual interviews, and tell me which of the two categories each interviewer falls into.'

It's a good exercise, and it illustrates an important point. If you're hoping to spot patterns in a person's behaviour, it helps to know in advance what sorts of patterns to look for.

You should be striving to build up a catalogue of commonly found patterns that you can store away and draw upon as you're talking with a particular candidate. Start with one or two dimensions that you've come across before, or read about somewhere. Practise applying them to people until they've become second nature to you. Then add another one. And another one after that.

The Evaluation Question

There are a couple of special 'techniques' you can use to help you detect patterns in a candidate's behaviour and translate them into meaningful personality terms. The first of these is the *Evaluation Question*.

The Evaluation Question involves asking the *candidate* to come up with hypotheses about his or her own behaviour. It invites the candidate to explore the real meaning of something that has happened. To look at the 'why' or the 'how' of a specific event.

A couple of examples.

You're interviewing a young graduate who has informed you that they had been elected head prefect during their final year at school. A good Evaluation Question might be:

'What qualities do you think your classmates recognised in you that caused them to elect you head prefect?'

Or, suppose the candidate has built up an excellent track record in a number of previous selling jobs. A good Evaluation Question might be:

'What is there about your approach to selling, do you think, that would account for the success that you appear to have had so far in your selling career?'

Finally, imagine talking to a candidate who has changed jobs often enough during the past several years to make you think it might mean something. You might ask:

'Let's see, Frank, you've had three, four, five jobs in the past ten years...do you think there's any reason why you've moved around so much?'

> Invite the applicant to go beyond the reported facts and look at the underlying traits or factors at work.

Asked in a genuinely open-minded way, and used with a fair degree of selectivity, the Evaluation Question can be a powerful interviewing tool. It invites the applicant to go beyond the reported facts and look at the underlying traits or factors at work. It asks them to stop and think – really *think* about their own strengths, weaknesses, values, and operating style.

By doing so, it presents a number of advantages to you, the interviewer.

♦ It helps you formulate hypotheses.
♦ It prevents jumping to conclusions.
♦ It stimulates genuine introspection.

It helps you formulate hypotheses

We talked earlier about the need to develop hypotheses about the candidate's skills and attributes as they are talking. The need is to relate the 'facts' of the candidate's background to the core dimensions which we are trying to evaluate. The Evaluation Question helps us do that. It gives us the candidate's view of what the facts mean – of what skills and attributes underlie the specific experience and events in his or her background.

It prevents jumping to conclusions

Asking the Evaluation Question is a good way of making sure that we know how and *why* the candidate has done what he or she has done.

It is all too easy to assume, for example, that graduating near the top of one's class means that the candidate is very intelligent. In actual fact, the posing of an Evaluation Question might reveal that the candidate did so well simply because they worked harder – or because the class as a whole was a mediocre one.

It stimulates genuine introspection

Most applicants have been interviewed before, and many have become quite good at it. It is fairly easy for the 'experienced' interviewee to run through their background in a very articulate fashion without once stopping to really *think*.

The Evaluation Question helps prevent this. It forces the candidate to stop and reflect. By doing so, it reduces the likelihood of your being unduly impressed by sheer articulation alone.

Be prepared to probe

When you ask people to tell you about their strengths and weaknesses, or to simply evaluate themselves in some other way, the answer you get is very likely to be broad and generalised to the point of being meaningless.

A person might say something like: 'I'm always looking for an opportunity to learn' and 'I've always been a pretty ambitious person' and that 'money is important to me but what really matters is the personal satisfaction I get from doing the job' and that 'I don't like the idea of just maintaining a territory...I need a chance to really *build* something'.

The way these statements roll off the person's tongue, usually just dripping in sincerity, you can usually tell that they have been well rehearsed. They're 'stock answers'.

But don't hold that against the candidate. It is preferable to hear stock answers from someone who's taken the trouble to prepare them than to sit and listen to someone ramble on incoherently.

The *real* trouble is that these answers don't in fact tell us very much. They're so full of broad generalities and textbook clichés that it's hard to put much stock in their content.

> The *real* trouble is that these answers don't in fact tell us very much.

There are a couple of reasons why this happens:

♦ Because people think that way. A lot of people simply aren't very good at analysing themselves crisply and incisively. They *think* in broad generalities, and don't spend a lot of time on introspection in the first place.

♦ Because they're on guard. They want to make a good impression. Some people do it all the time, even to themselves. Other people just do it in the interview, because there's an important job at stake and the way to get it is to make a 'good' impression.

Either way, you have to be careful when you ask people for their broad evaluation of themselves. Always dig a little bit with some good follow-up probes.

'Aggressive is a pretty broad word, Larry – what do you mean when you say you're aggressive? How might it show up, for example, in the way you manage people, or the way you handle staff meetings?'

What you're trying to do is break beyond the semantic barrier that is always there when you're talking about people's 'personalities' – and bring things down to a behavioural level where you can get the data out on the table and decide for yourself whether the person really is 'aggressive' or not.

Positive or negative evaluation questions?

It's not often that you hear the candidate say anything negative about themself when you ask a direct question.

'How did you get along with your last boss? How is it that you've changed jobs four times in the last seven years?'

When the candidate hears this type of question, they are quick to realise that it's an important one, and that the answer is going to be looked at very carefully. Candidates are pretty *smart* – it's best to operate on that assumption. So the candidate will give you an answer that seems reasonably intelligent and logical and puts them in as positive a light as possible. That's just human nature.

Negative characteristics are more likely to be mentioned

when the candidate feels confident than when they feel threatened.

The candidate will feel more confident when they are encouraged to talk about positive things. The more they have a chance to talk about the good things they have accomplished, the more likely it is that they will go a bit further and mention some of the things that are *not* so positive.

Most of your Evaluation Questions, therefore, should be of the positive variety – especially during the initial stages of the interview.

'You were able to turn around the division a lot more quickly than anyone had anticipated...What do you think accounted for that?'

'So, at the tender age of 32, you were given responsibility for the total engineering department. What is it about you, or your performance, do you think, that led to your being selected for the role?'

Once you've asked a few of these positive Evaluation Questions, you're in a position to begin probing a bit for the person's shortcomings. Even here, though, try to do it in a fundamentally positive and accepting manner.

The Shared Hypothesis

I mentioned *two* techniques. Number two is what we'll call the *Shared Hypothesis*.

There's no better way of taking a tentative hypothesis that you've drawn up in your own mind – and checking it out, confirming it, or fine-tuning it – than by putting it out on the table and seeing what the candidate's reaction is.

'You know, John, when I hear you talking about the way you handled yourself in that meeting, and the way you manage your own work group, it seems to me that you're not quite as aggressive as the job you're doing seems to call for.'

Or:

'I'll tell you what I'm concerned about at this stage, Jill. I see a lot of good traits in you, and I can see why you've made the progress

that you've made over the past few years. But I have a hunch that you're a bit too much the "entrepreneur" to really be happy in this job.'

The sharing of hypotheses is an advanced technique, in terms of both how much skill is involved and when it enters into the interviewing process. It needs to be used very carefully. The key is to form hypotheses in a tentative manner and then share them with the candidate in a tentative way that encourages a non-defensive, exploratory response.

You're not *accusing* the candidate of anything. You're simply asking for his or her help in deciding whether a conclusion that's starting to emerge is one that holds water.

It's a very potent technique, especially when it's combined with *Follow-up Probes*, as we see in this example:

'As you've been talking, George, I've been thinking to myself — Boy, he's really an aggressive sort of individual. When he wants something, he sure doesn't beat around the bush; he just puts his head down and goes after it. That's true, isn't it?'

And George, at that point, will probably think about that for a minute and then come back with something like:

'Yeah, I think that's very true of me. I don't think it's a question of being aggressive so much as it's a matter of knowing what I want. Once I know what I'm after, I get impatient with people or with things that get in my way.'

And that gives you a perfect opportunity to carry things a little further and say to George:

'Doesn't that get you into trouble at times? I mean, I know people who know what they're after — and they usually end up getting it — but they don't go around knocking people over or barrelling through them. They're tactful. And patient.'

And then George will probably keep the ball rolling, and come right back with something like:

'Yeah, I know what you mean. I guess I'm just not built that way. I don't believe in pussyfooting around or trying to be diplomatic just because other people are too scared or too bloody lazy to get off their rear ends and do something.'

Ah ha! I think we know now what sort of person we're dealing with. Let's try this on for size:

'Well, okay George. But what would you do if, let's say, you were pushing for something in a staff meeting and the Chairman says "Okay, I think we've talked this one through pretty well and we're still at loggerheads... let's shelve it for now and put it back on the agenda for next week". How would you handle that sort of situation?'

You can see what's happening. And where the conversation is leading. You're getting a handle on one particular aspect of George's personality, checking it out with him, and then seeing how it might show up in situations of the sort that he'll probably have to deal with if he's hired into the new job.

This underscores the importance of generating hypotheses *during* the interview rather than after the fact. Even if we don't share our hypotheses openly with the candidate, we can still work to validate and fine-tune them in the interview by searching for confirmatory evidence in the form of additional behavioural examples.

A note on note-taking

Once the interview has been concluded, and the candidate has gone, it is essential that you have some record of what was discussed, what was learned, and what was decided.

And there is no substitute here for the taking of effective notes. A good interviewer does not rely on memory alone as a means of recording and storing the data. They take notes – both while the interview is in progress and immediately after its conclusion.

Not everyone would agree with this, mind you. There are, in fact, two objections to note-taking which are commonly voiced. One is that the introduction of note-taking during the interview tends to create tension and caution in the person being interviewed. The other is that the taking of notes makes it difficult for the interviewer to really concentrate on what is being said. Let's examine both of these arguments.

It generates tension and caution

This, in actual fact, depends on *how* the notes are taken. If the candidate can easily see what is being written down, or if the notes are taken only when they say something negative – then anxiety and wariness are almost inevitable.

The best way to take notes is to do so evenly and unobtrusively. Keep the pad on your lap rather than on the desk, and take notes consistently but not constantly throughout the course of the interview.

It prevents genuine concentration

This needn't be the case. An experienced interviewer learns to take notes naturally and automatically, without removing their attention from the candidate and without failing to hear the real meaning of what is being said.

This comes with practice. The best approach is to record only very brief notes – you soon develop a form of shorthand which you and only you can decipher – and record only those things which are important, rather than making a vain effort to capture every word or phrase that is uttered.

List the facts and hypotheses

One approach is to take a blank pad of lined paper and draw a line down the middle. That gives us two columns: one on the left for *Facts* and one on the right for *hypotheses*.

There should be relatively little written on the *Facts* side of the form as compared to the *hypotheses* side. There is no reason to record things which are already available on the application form or CV, for example.

Concentrate, rather, on writing down those things which the candidate has done or said which you feel are significant. Look for specific events, actions, decisions, or experiences which you feel have a lot to say about the candidate's skills and attributes.

Most of your note-taking should take place on the *hypotheses* side of the interviewing form. One source of hypotheses will be your actual observations during the interview:

◆ Communicates clearly.
◆ Relates easily to strangers.
◆ Gets lost in detail.
◆ Slow to grasp things.

Another main source will, of course, be your own interpretations of the 'facts' being presented. We also have the candidate's own self-evaluations as a third very fruitful source of hypotheses.

The main point to remember, for now, is that the experienced interviewer is doing a lot more than simply gathering 'facts'. They are weighing these facts, listening for their true meaning, spotting the patterns behind them, and translating those patterns into predictions about on-the-job behaviour. They are, in sort, developing *hypotheses*. And it is these hypotheses – not the facts on which they are based – that hold the real secret to effective hiring.

Summary

In this chapter we have looked at how we move from dealing with specifics to the general. How we can use the facts of Behavioural Patterns to help us predict general future performance.

We conduct selection interviews on two levels:

◆ The first is the *factual* level where facts like background, current situation, experiences, decisions, thoughts, feelings, ideas, actions or reactions are discussed and probed in depth.

◆ The second is the *inferential* level where the Behavioural Patterns identified from the first level are used to predict on-the-job-performance. We translate facts into hypotheses.

◆ Let's get to know the personality of the candidate we're interviewing and not be blinded by too many facts.

Ask the candidate to evaluate their own behaviour in a specific situation:

◆ It helps you form your hypotheses.
◆ It prevents you from jumping to conclusions.

- It stimulates genuine introspection.

- Be prepared to probe and use positive evaluation questions whenever possible.

- Don't be afraid to check out your hypotheses with the candidate during the interview. Used carefully, this is a good method of measuring their behaviour when making a prediction about themselves. Particularly if they're aware it's balanced against previous behavioural patterns.

- Beware of too much note-taking. You must make some notes but don't create unnecessary stress or tension in the candidate – especially when they think they've said something negative. Remember that it can also prevent genuine concentration on your part.

We use the Interview Checklist to get our final thoughts about the candidate down on paper.

Have We Got a Winner?

The interview with Susan is over. You have three other people to see in quick succession. Or, there's a meeting you should have been in five minutes ago and then a scheduled lunch with someone from the Logistics area. Either way, you've got a busy day ahead of you.

There's a rule we should establish right here and now. *At the end of every interview, allow five minutes for note-taking.*

What do we do with our five minutes? We take notes. If we don't do it now, we'll probably *never* do it. Of, if we try to do it later in the day, things that seem clear and fresh and important in our mind now will have disappeared. So let's stick to the rule of allowing five minutes at the end of every interview.

> At the end of every interview, allow five minutes for note-taking. Follow this rule religiously. Don't deviate from it.

Our purpose in this chapter is to take a closer look at the *Interview Checklist* – a system you can use to record your thoughts about the candidate. (See Figure 5.)

Why a checklist?

Why a checklist? Why not just a blank pad of paper?

A checklist forces us to *attend* to certain things. It puts those things on the agenda. If *Took the initiative in steering the discussion into specific areas* is one of the items on our checklist, then we have to keep our eyes open during the interview for this specific sort of behaviour. If we didn't have the checklist, or if we had one but this item wasn't *on* it, then we might not notice this specific sort of behaviour.

So the idea is to have a checklist and to include on it the things that *count*. We have used the same list as that used for the Winner's Profile.

◆ GOAL ORIENTATION – Is the candidate ambitious? Have they set themselves a goal? How have they planned for it?

◆ ORGANISATION – Is there a record of systematic organisation?

◆ INITIATIVE – How did they achieve things? How was success achieved?

◆ INTELLIGENCE – Is the candidate quick on the uptake as well as being bright?

◆ RELATIONSHIP-BUILDING – Is the candidate easy to get to know?

◆ COMMUNICATION SKILLS – Does the candidate communicate in a straightforward manner? Do they get to the point quickly?

◆ LEADERSHIP – How does the candidate have authority? Can they remain focused and unruffled?

◆ ENTHUSIASM – Is the candidate fun to work with? Do they enjoy the work?

◆ DRIVE – Does the candidate have a determination to excel?

◆ RESILIENCE – How has the candidate dealt with failure?

◆ SELF-DEVELOPMENT – How has the candidate made themself more effective?

◆ STAYABILITY – Is the candidate going to stay long enough to repay our investment in them?

Fig. 5. Interview Checklist.

We have agreed that we will take both a *targeted* and a *behavioural* approach to the interview. We will target specific aspects of the person's make-up, skill set, or operating style and we will look for *behavioural* evidence that those things are in fact there.

The checklist helps us to do both. It says, in effect, here are the specific things we are targeting in this interview and here are some specific behaviours that you should look for in order to assess where the candidate stands.

So the *Interview Checklist*, when all is said and done, is absolutely crucial. It is a very direct way of putting our overall strategy for the interview into practice.

Thinking like a customer

As we go through the checklist, we are going to pay particular attention to how we use the candidate's behaviour *right there in the interview* as an important source of data. You may recall what we said about *thinking like a customer.* We have to assume that how the candidate behaves in the interview is representative of how they behave generally, and how they would behave when face-to-face with a colleague or customer. There is no reason to assume otherwise. So – we think like a customer, and size the candidate up in the exact same way that a colleague or customer would do it. We pay attention to what we see and what we hear.

1. Goal Orientation

Winners are decisive, disciplined goal-setters. They make clear decisions about what they want and then go after it in a disciplined and well-orchestrated fashion.

- They develop the habit of setting specific and meaningful goals for themself.
- They pin their goals down in clear, precise terms. They know exactly what they're after.
- They set goals which are realistically attainable – but which involve a definite 'stretch'.
- They develop a specific action plan that tells how each goal will be achieved.
- They attach a specific target date to each goal whenever possible and appropriate.
- They keep their plans out in the open. They serve as a guide to day-to-day decision-making.

It's not enough to know that a candidate is *ambitious.* Most reasonably good people are ambitious, and all candidates are smart enough to know that they should at the very least *describe* themselves as ambitious if asked.

The more important question is whether the candidate really *works* at it. And working at it begins with the setting of clear, specific goals. Look at the achievements of successful people and you will find that they knew what they were after. They set a clear, specific goal for themselves. They wrote it down. They attached a target to it. They knew precisely what they wanted to accomplish.

> *Winners* are decisive, disciplined goal-setters. They make clear decisions about what they want and then go after it in a disciplined and well-orchestrated fashion.

Get them to explain their goal

You will find, too, that they had a *plan* for achieving the goal. They didn't expect to achieve it through some combination of hard work and good luck and persistence. They translated the goal into a logical, comprehensive plan with specific action steps linked together logically within a workable time schedule.

Moreover, it becomes clear that goal-setting is a general *habit* that applies as much to their personal lives as to their business lives. They don't just decide that they'd like to own a lakeside cottage or have lots of money put aside for the future. They set specific goals. They know what kind of cottage, how much it will cost, and when they are going to buy it. They know how much money they want to have in their savings or investment account and when they want to have it.

It might not happen exactly the way it was set out in their goal...but they know that, if they don't have a specific goal with a specific target date attached to it, it probably *won't happen at all.*

Give extra marks, by the way, to the person who *writes* their goals down. Experience shows that ideas floating around in one's head seldom amount to much more than daydreams, while things that are written down on paper are acted upon and get done.

2. Organisation

The second quality that we'll be looking for in this initial interview is *Organisation.*

◆ They plan their day systematically and know what has to be done and in what order.
◆ They write down what specific goals have to be accomplished during the day.
◆ They talk in an organised way and make a point logically and systematically.
◆ They go into meetings and presentations well prepared and

with a clear plan in mind.

♦ They came to the interview well prepared and had taken time to do their homework.

♦ They demonstrate the ability to plan, organise, and execute a major project.

Put simply, we need to know that Susan is an organised person who gets things done – and pursues her goals – in a systematic, intelligent, and effective manner.

We'll look at two things: how she has organised things in the past, both on the job and off, and how she has gone about organising herself for *this interview.*

Intelligent execution. This is a person who executes in an intelligent and effective manner. This is what we have to be able to say about a candidate. No matter what the task, they must analyse the situation, set specific goals, think through the strategy for pursuing those goals, develop a specific plan of action, and execute a plan in a disciplined, focused and ultimately effective manner. There is no wasted effort, no scrambling at the last minute to get things done.

3. Initiative

Initiative is something we generally recognise when we see it. The person takes the bull by the horns and moves into action without being prodded or given the go-ahead. They do what has to be done, even if it means doing something a bit out of the ordinary or taking a course of action that's going to raise the boss's eyebrows a bit. They don't dawdle. They don't play it safe. They don't fall back on the routine or accepted or authorised way of handling things. They do what's needed to solve the problem to achieve the result. And they do it promptly.

♦ They have a strong sense of urgency – keenly aware of the need to move quickly on things.

♦ They seem to move into action promptly and decisively when a problem arises.

♦ They keep on top of things, follow through, make sure that things get done.

♦ They show a willingness to cut through red tape in order to

move things ahead.
- They show initiative – taking the bull by the horns and dealing with things.
- They show a consistent pattern of independent decision-making and action-taking.

This is one area that clearly requires us to look at the person's achievements – both on the job and off – and dig for the specifics of *how* they achieved things. *Initiative* is not something that we will see directly in the interview itself. We have to look closely – *behaviourally* – at the candidate's major achievements and more specifically at how they acted when an unexpected problem cropped up or an unexpected opportunity arose. When there was no 'routine' way of handling things, when independent decision-making or action-taking was required, did the candidate *deal* with the situation?

That's the acid test. That's the pattern of behaviour that we are looking for.

4. Intelligence

The next item is *Intelligence*. Increasingly to do an effective job, a person has to have at least an average level of intelligence. If you take a close look at your top performers, you will probably find that they are quick, perceptive thinkers who size things up deftly and are quick to see what is happening in a situation or where a discussion is leading. Good at grasping what the other person is trying to say. Quick to spot a flaw in the other person's logic, to see an opportunity unfolding, or to come up with the answer to a problem.

- Their education suggests that they are comfortably above-average in intelligence.
- They successfully handled complex products with complex applications.
- They were thinking during the interview. They were mentally alert, quick on the up-take.
- They seem quick to grasp what is being said and where the discussion is going.
- They cut quickly to the heart of a question or issue, and see what's crucial and what's not.

♦ They seem to have a good vocabulary and use words that are not used by most people.

This isn't intelligence *per se*, at least not in the sense of the person having an eye-catching *IQ* score. It's *ground-level* intelligence. It's quickness, flexibility, and agility. It's the ability to think effectively *on one's feet*.

And it is this sort of intelligence that we need to see in any candidate that we consider bringing on board.

How do they behave?

Once again, a good way to assess this is to look at the person's behaviour right there in the interview. Does Susan think quickly on her feet? Does she grasp what you are asking — quickly, accurately, and without having to have it spelled out in detail? Is she alert? Does she pick out the essential part of a question, and zero in on it? Does she see and respond to the *gist* of what you were asking even when you rambled a bit or your question turned out to be a bit clumsy?

Or — is she slow to grasp things? Does she visibly pause to digest a question before responding to it... almost to the point where her brow gets furrowed and you can hear the wheels grinding away? Does she respond only to the *first* part of a two-part question, suggesting that she has either forgotten about the second part or wasn't able to take it in? Does she take what you say too *literally*, responding to the letter of a question but not to the spirit?

Does she ask intelligent *questions*? Does she ask equally intelligent *follow-up* questions which show that she has actually thought about the answer you gave and is building upon it? Do you get a sense that she is thinking about what you are saying, responding to it, taking it further. Do you get a sense that *this is an intelligent, thoughtful individual*?

When all is said and done, the main thing to look for is evidence that the candidate is *thinking* during the interview. Thinking as opposed to giving out pat answers and sticking to the prepared text. When a person is *thinking*, when they are really and truly thinking, you will know it. You will get an unmistakable sense that things are *happening* during the interview, that it is turning into something more than an exchange of stock questions and pat answers.

> The main thing to look for is evidence that the candidate is *thinking* during the interview.

Again – *think like a customer.* You know what your needs and priorities are... Is this person bright enough to deliver?

5. Relationship-building

We will be assessing this in regard to the candidate's *Education, Work History,* and *Personal Life and Hobbies.* In many ways, however, the best evidence to a person's being able to build good relationships is the sort of impact they make on *you* during the interview. For one thing, the candidate should be *easy to talk to* – at ease, relaxed, comfortable, not self-conscious or inhibited or cautious and ill-at-ease. If you were meeting such a person for the first time, at a party, you wouldn't have to 'make conversation' with them. It would flow naturally.

◆ I enjoyed talking with this person. I can easily imagine making friends with them.
◆ They have a friendly manner – cheerful, outgoing, positive, glad to see you.
◆ They seem to be socially active and to have quite a wide circle of friends.
◆ They seem to have built good relationships with their colleagues and/or customers.
◆ They have got to know colleagues and customers on something more than just a business basis.
◆ They are easy to talk to – relaxed, able to make small talk and keep a conversation going.

Look for signs, too, that the person exercises basic social skills, that they are at ease in social situations, at ease with people, good at making small talk and putting other people at ease, a good conversationalist, good at drawing people out or using a nod of the head to express interest and encourage the other person to say more.

And... ask yourself a simple question – is the individual

personable? Is the person someone you enjoyed talking to? Could you imagine yourself becoming friends with this person after a short time of working together? Don't be afraid to trust your instincts here. It's safe to assume that most other people will respond to this person in more or less the same way you did.

One last thing – and it's very important. A candidate should be *straightforward.* One of the things that we know about our top sales performers is that they are honest and up-front with customers. And you should get the same sort of feeling about the candidate that you are interviewing. You should sense that the person is relaxed, being themselves, not putting on a show or playing out a role, not trying to 'sell' themselves to you, not self-conscious. You should get a sense that what you are seeing is a *real person.*

Notice how we are using *your* reactions to the candidate as an important measure of what they have to offer. There's nothing wrong with that. If you liked the person, or *didn't* like the person, there's a good chance that your customers will react in precisely the same way.

What you are doing, in effect, is putting yourself in your colleagues' and customers' shoes and assessing this person on their behalf. Is the person *likeable?* Is this the sort of person with whom you could become friends, or work with closely? Was there a good *rapport* between the two of you during the interview – and was the candidate's behaviour instrumental in *building* that rapport?

6. Communication Skills

We need to know that the individual has the good basic *Communication Skills* that are going to be required in a selling role. And the most logical way to assess that is to look for those skills right there in the interview.

- ◆ They communicated ideas clearly and succinctly during the interview.
- ◆ They stopped periodically to make sure we were on the same wavelength.
- ◆ They used words effectively – using the right word or phrase in the right spot.

◆ They talk in an interesting fashion. They are interesting to listen to.
◆ Difficult or awkward questions were handled smoothly, They didn't get flustered.
◆ They listen well, paying attention and work hard to understand.

What do we mean by good communication skills? Firstly, we have to look at how the person *talks*, and ask ourselves whether they are not just talking freely but *communicating effectively.* Do they say things in a straightforward, no-nonsense manner or is their speech needlessly flowery and ornate? Do they get to the point quickly, or is there a tendency to ramble and get side-tracked? Do they use words accurately and appropriately, or do they over-rely on clichés and general words or phrases that don't quite fit? When all is said and done, do they get the message through? Are they effective communicators?

And – does the person *listen* effectively? Do we see active, genuine listening? Do they pick up on things, check for understanding, ask us to clarify or repeat something that wasn't quite clear, and ask intelligent follow-up questions that show that really they have been listening?

Pay attention, finally, to how the person gathers information. One way to look at it is to ask yourself whether the candidate is doing a good job of interviewing *you.* Using *Probes,* for example. Give good marks to the candidate who probes for relevant details, asks you to elaborate on something you've said, and asks intelligent follow-up questions that show that he or she has really been listening.

7. Leadership

Part of what we're calling *Leadership* has to do with how clearly and how firmly one expresses one's opinions. Look for signs during the interview that the candidate is comfortable saying what's on their mind. Do they state facts and opinions in a confident and authoritative manner, for example, or do they seem tentative, hesitant, or even apologetic? Are they definite in their beliefs and unambiguous in their opinions, or are they vague and wishy-washy?

- They seemed confident and sure of themself during the interview.
- They stated facts and opinions in a confident and authoritative way during the interview.
- More than once, they took the initiative in steering the discussion into a specific area.
- They gave evidence of being willing to challenge or interrupt in an appropriate way.
- They took the initiative in raising the *What happens next?* issue at the end of the interview.
- At various points in their life, they have been selected for a leadership role.

There are *other* signs of leadership and assertiveness that we can look for in the interview. For example – an assertive person, someone with leadership ability, will gently interrupt you at least once during the interview in order to complete a thought or make a point. It will be done gracefully and perhaps with a bit of humour... but it will be done.

And that same person will *resist* being interrupted or side-tracked. If you jump in and interrupt something they are saying, they will be gracious about it. They won't just keep talking. But, when you've made your point or got out what you wanted to say, they'll go back to where they were before the interruption. And they'll do it by saying something like this –

'Yes, I can see the point you're making, and I think it's a good one. Now...let me return for a minute to what I was saying earlier about my role on the NPD committee...'

As you can see, what we're calling *Leadership* has very much to do with *how* we say things, what exact words we use, and when we use them. And this underscores the importance of taking a *behavioural* approach to the interview and using our *Probe* and *Follow-up* tools to dig for specifics. We need to get the candidate to describe exactly what happened in a situation. Who said what to whom, and in what tone of voice?

We're looking for *Leadership* of the sort that a top salesperson might demonstrate during a sales call – steering the discussion, guiding it gently toward a decision point, challenging something the customer has said, being proactive, taking responsibility for moving things ahead and getting things accomplished, taking active steps to solicit an action commitment or arrange for the next step in the selling cycle.

And these are exactly the sorts of things that you should look for *in the interview*. Does the candidate do these sorts of things in his or her discussion with you?

And – in your discussions of the candidate's background – do you see evidence of them having exercised this sort of leadership?

8. Enthusiasm

What we are looking for here is evidence that the candidate is an enthusiastic sort of person who gets enthusiastically involved in whatever they are doing and who has *Enthusiasm* – especially in regard to their *goals*.

◆ There is a 'sparkle' in their eyes when they talk. There is *Enthusiasm* showing through.
◆ You can tell from their voice that they are enthusiastic.
◆ They express enthusiasm about the job – and about this company as an employer.
◆ They express enthusiasm about previous jobs, products, or employers.
◆ It is clear that they really and truly enjoy what they do.
◆ On at least one occasion, *Enthusiasm* was what allowed them to achieve results.

We want to know that they are enthusiastic for the simple reason that successful people are enthusiastic. *Winners* are fun people to be with. They enjoy their work and they enjoy life and they enjoy other people. They are enthusiastic people.

How do we know whether a person is enthusiastic? Ask yourself how you know that a person is enthusiastic, and you'll probably find that it comes from two types of evidence: their *eyes* and their *voice*. So – we listen to what our eyes and ears are telling us. Enthusiastic people talk in an animated manner. Their voice goes up and down to lend emphasis to what

> *Winners* are fun people to be with. They enjoy their work and they enjoy life and they enjoy other people.

they're saying. Their eyes seem to sparkle when they talk about what they're involved in. They *radiate* – there's no better word for it – something almost tangible which most of us should be able to recognise when we see it.

So – it's not something we *delve* for by asking questions. It's something we *observe*.

Still, there are times when you might want to throw in not so much a question as a *reflective* comment.

'I don't sense you were very enthusiastic about that particular part of your job...'

If she says '*No, I wasn't*' and then goes on to explain why, then you've learned something. If, on the other hand, Susan protests and says that yes, she *was* enthusiastic about that aspect of her job, then you've learned something else. Either she doesn't *display* her enthusiasm – it doesn't come through in her manner of talking – or else what she calls *enthusiasm* is more of an intellectual quality than an emotional one.

In either case, treat it as cause for concern and probe for the same sort of thing later on in the interview. The sort of enthusiasm that we find in successful people is very much an *emotional* quality, not an intellectual one, and it is very much *displayed* in their manner.

9. Drive

In order for you to decide to invite a candidate back for a second interview, you have to come away from the *first* interview with a clear, unmistakable sense that the person you are dealing with is an *achiever*.

- They set their sights high, not settling for 'average' or 'satisfactory' results.
- There is evidence that they have displayed tenacity in the pursuit of their goals.
- In at least one situation, they stuck with something when most people would have given up.
- They enjoy competitive sports, and they enjoy them because they are competitive.
- There is an intensity about this person. You sense it when you talk to them.

♦ They have excelled. They have succeeded in being the very best in what they do.

A *Winner* is someone who aims high, who aims for *achievement*, because that's the way they're built. It's something they carry around inside them. A determination to excel. A desire to be the very best that they can be. A fundamental *competitiveness* of the sort that one always finds – *always* – in a champion racehorse or a Super Bowl quarterback.

> A *Winner* is someone who aims high, who aims for *achievement*, because that's the way they're built. It's something they carry around inside them. A determination to excel.

Can this sort of thing be *assessed?* Can it be assessed in a *first interview?*

Only in part. *Drive* is one of those qualities that is so broad and runs so deep that it is difficult to get a complete handle on it. What we have to aim for is an overall sense that the person sitting across from us is an *achiever* whose achievements are spurred on by some sort of inner need to achieve. We can't open the person up and look at that inner quality *directly*, but we have to get a pretty good sense that it's *there*.

So we ask ourselves – *What do people with Drive do? What is it about them that tells us that they have lots of Drive?*

Well, they usually like competitive sports, for one thing – and this is something we alluded to in our discussion during the *Personal Life and Hobbies* portion of the interview.

The importance of being focused

What *else* do people with *Drive* do? They stick with a goal until it has been achieved. That's something they do. They are tenacious. They don't give up. They are *focused*. They don't drift off to something easier just because their main objective is proving to be a bit more difficult than they had anticipated. They grit their teeth and dig their heels in and redouble their efforts.

Do we see signs of that sort of tenacity in how the candidate has gone about things? What we have to do is look in detail at how they went about pursuing an objective – it can come from their educational background, or it might be a goal that they were pursuing at *work*, or it could be something that has to do with one of their hobbies…it can be within *any* of the areas that we'll be covering in the first interview – and get a feel for just how much determination and tenacity were involved in its pursuit. Whether the goal was actually *achieved* or not is not the crucial thing; it's what went *into* it.

This is where our *Probing* and *Follow-Up* tools become so important. We use them to dig for the details.

◆ *What exactly was the obstacle you faced?*
◆ *How did you feel about things at that stage?*
◆ *What exactly did you do to get around the obstacle?*
◆ *When exactly did you do that?*

There's no way to get at something as diffuse as *Drive* or 'tenacity' except by digging for the details of what the situation was, what went through the candidate's mind, what they *did* to get around the obstacle or solve the problem, and how long it took them to do it.

We have to look for evidence that candidates have been tenacious – have displayed tenacity in their actual *behaviour* – in the past. Evidence that at various times in the past, or indeed as a matter of habit, they have been striving toward well-defined goals with a great deal of determination and have, therefore, achieved the goals that they have established for themselves. If they haven't achieved the goals, it needn't imply that they haven't been tenacious – but one ought to see a *pattern* of achievement.

> We have to look for evidence that candidates have been tenacious – have displayed tenacity in their actual *behaviour* – in the past.

10. Resilience

Is the candidate the kind of person who rebounds quickly after a setback, who has learned to deal maturely with problems and obstacles and frustrations?

◆ They have shown evidence of being able to rebound following a serious setback.

◆ They have *experienced* adversity and have not had a life where everything has come easily.

◆ On at least one occasion they have shown that they are able to take criticism and learn from it.

◆ They are able to leave problems behind at the end of the day and don't *dwell* on things.

◆ They don't get discouraged or dispirited when results are slow in coming.

◆ *Self-confidence* is one of the specific strengths they mentioned when asked.

If there have been no problems or obstacles or frustrations to deal with, if there have been no failures, then it's unlikely that Susan has the make-up needed to be an outstanding performer. The sorts of people who become top performers are people who have aimed high – not those who have settled for average. And people who aim high are not going to succeed all the time. They will have had their share of setbacks and failures.

Try, in the interview, to talk in some detail about at least one major failure or setback or hardship. Something Susan had attempted – and failed. Or, if need be, simply a very trying experience such as the loss of a loved one or the loss of a job.

What happened next? That's the important question. What did she do *following* the event? Did she rebound quickly, and get on with things? Did she *learn* from the experience? Put it to good use? Did it change the way she handled things in the future? Did it make her a more mature person? Did it alter her view of things?

We said that successful people will have not only had their share of setbacks and failures. They will *also* have made their share of *mistakes*. Successful people are not people who shy away from making mistakes. They *expect* to make mistakes, and they respond to those mistakes by using them as opportunities for learning and personal growth.

A candidate should be able to talk openly and confidently

about the mistakes that they have made along the way. Good candidates will have taken time to analyse each situation. They will know what was *right* about their approach and where they miscalculated, and they won't spend a lot of time blaming other people or external events. Their focus is on what *they* themselves could or should have done to produce a better result.

11. Self-development

To appreciate how important *Self-development* is, we just have to look around us – at some of the outstanding people we work with. *Winners* are always looking for an extra edge. They are always studying themselves. They see themselves as tools for the accomplishment of results. They are always thinking about their own effectiveness, turning to self-help books for insight and tools, analysing their own performance, trying to improve upon it, trying to anticipate what new knowledge and skills will be needed to maintain a competitive edge in *tomorrow's* selling environment.

- They have demonstrated the ability to analyse their own mistakes and learn from them.
- They have demonstrated the habit of analysing every sales call and learning from it.
- They have, and can articulate, specific self-development goals toward which they are working.
- They can identify in what specific ways they have improved during the past twelve months.
- They welcome feedback on their own performance and take active steps to solicit it.
- They keep abreast of industry developments, new products, what the competition is doing.

Ask a top performer what they have done this past week to become more effective, and you will generally get a prompt, specific answer. Ask a poorer performer that same question, and there's a very good chance that you will draw a blank. Top salespeople don't take their own effectiveness for granted. They work on it day in and day out.

And, as is true of all they do, they go about it in a

disciplined, focused, results-driven fashion. They can tell you quite precisely what they are working on, and why, and how, and with what results.

It goes beyond just taking courses. Almost all candidates will include a list of courses and seminars on their CV, and the list – all by itself – doesn't tell you much. The key thing is *why* the courses were selected. The best courses are those which the candidate selected themselves, for very specific reasons. Not because they were made available or encouraged or offered or sponsored but because they were *needed* to enhance the person's effectiveness. If the candidate had to pay for the course out of their own pocket, so much the better.

So – one of the single most powerful questions we can ask of a candidate is not so much *What courses have you taken?* but *What, specifically, have you done during the past twelve months to increase your own effectiveness?*

You might want to ask that question of Susan. Directly. In just those words.

12. Stayability

The twelfth and final quality that we look for during the first interview is what we called *Stayability*. Will the person – *would* the person – stay with the company long enough to repay the considerable investment of time and money which we make in a new appointment?

- We have discussed our concerns about hiring good people and then having them leave.
- They have addressed those concerns, and we feel comfortable with how they have done that.
- They have a realistic view of the job – what's involved, what it will be like.
- They have a realistic view of the company and what it will be like to work here.
- Their long-term career aspirations can be realistically satisfied within this company.
- They have demonstrated a reluctance to 'hop' from one job to another without good reason.

This is a tough one. But you have to assess it. You're not

allowed to answer *I don't know.* You have to come up with a reasoned judgement regarding this *Stayability* factor – and it has to be done on the basis of things discussed or observed during the interview.

The question *What?* is an important one. *What* are the person's career goals? *What* is their perception of the job for which they are a candidate? *What* is their view of your company or organisation as a place to work?

Once you have, in your discussion with the candidate, got an answer to the question *What?* – then you can ask yourself how closely the answer matches reality. Are the candidate's career aspirations in line with the opportunities which the job contains? Is their perception of the job realistic? Are the things which they say are attractive about the job in fact *accurate?* When they talk about what they like about your company as a place to work, does it sound like the same company that *you* know?

Another important question is *Why?* Accepting that the candidate's perceptions are accurate, *why* does the job appeal to them? There *has* to be a reason, and there has to be a basic logic to it. If you stop and put yourself in the candidate's shoes, you should be able to see clearly why this job, and this company, make sense in terms of where you are in your career and where you are going.

If, when all is said and done, you have concerns, get them out on the table. Be totally candid.

'Mark, there's no question in my mind but that you could come in here and be a super performer. What I'm concerned about is whether or not we could hold on to you long enough to make it worthwhile.'

Be upfront about that. Put it out on the table as a problem that the two of you have to address and find an answer for.

Even if you *don't* have concerns, it's still not a bad idea to get the issue on the table anyway.

'Susan, one of my real concerns in bringing someone on board is how long they'll stay. The last thing in the world I want is to have you join us, do a bang-up job and then get head-hunted a year from now and leave because you can earn more working with the

competition. Any thoughts about that?'

Summary

In this chapter we have covered the importance of making notes after each interview and of using a checklist to look for specific examples of behaviour.

◆ We have used the same checklist as that used for the Winner's Profile.

◆ It focuses our thoughts on those things important to picking a winner both during and after the interview.

◆ It helps at this stage of the proceedings if we think like a customer when looking for patterns of behaviour.

The Winner's Profile is:

◆ Goal Orientation.

◆ Organisation.

◆ Initiative.

◆ Intelligence.

◆ Relationship-building.

◆ Communication Skills.

◆ Leadership.

◆ Enthusiasm.

◆ Drive.

◆ Resilience.

◆ Self-development.

◆ Stayability.

CHAPTER 21

Making the Decision

L et's tackle the *big* question. Do we *hire* this person? To the novice interviewer, this final step in the interviewing process always appears to be the most complex and mysterious. Oddly enough, though, it's actually the easiest step of all. So easy, in fact, that people are often baffled because they *expect* it to be a lot more complicated.

> We take what we have learned about the candidate and project it into the future.

It involves *visualising* how the candidate will perform if hired. What this means is that we take what we have learned about the candidate and project it into the future. And that's basically all that's involved. You simply project the person ahead, in your mind's eye, into the new job.

Not logically. Or analytically. But *visually.* Close your eyes and imagine the candidate handling the Tuesday marketing meeting, or giving a presentation to the purchasing people over at W. S. Tyler, or handling the telephone call that Frank had to deal with last Tuesday.

Project them into situations that you can actually visualise – that you've seen handled before by other people or have had to deal with yourself. Create the future, in your mind's eye, as vividly and as realistically as you can. As if you were actually *there.*

I can just see it now

Sounds crazy? Well, try this on for size. Imagine two people sitting over coffee in the company cafeteria, talking about a mutual acquaintance – someone they both know quite well and have observed in action in quite a number of different situations.

The first person chuckles to himself and says to the second, '*I hear Frank's been put in charge of the Budget Committee . . . that's a laugh*'.

And the second, also chuckling to himself now as he imagines Frank carrying out this new assignment, says:

'*Yeah, I can just see it now . . . Jim'll tell him to take his six per cent ceiling and shove it and then Frank'll get all red in the face and start stammering and ask Jim exactly where he'd like it shoved and how hard.*'

Visualising future performance, in this fashion, is something we do all the time – in a wide variety of situations. When we say '*Yeah, I can just see it now*', that's precisely what we mean.

> Visualising future performance, in this fashion, is something we do all the time – in a wide variety of situations.

We can actually 'see' the person's behaviour and 'hear' the person's voice – even though we're talking about a situation that hasn't happened yet. And may never happen, for all we know.

We can project their performance

Now why is that? How is it that we're able to conjure up such a vivid and life-like image of something that doesn't exist?

The answer is obvious. It's because we *know* the person in question. We know the person in the sense of having watched them perform in the past, heard the voice, noticed the mannerisms, seen the reaction to this or that type of event, observed the way they handle various situations or deal with various types of people.

And, because we've seen enough of their behaviour to detect some underlying patterns and consistencies in it, we're pretty confident when we project these patterns ahead into the future. So confident, in fact, that we do it automatically. Without even thinking about it.

And there's no reason on earth why we should not be able to do this very same thing with a candidate. True, we haven't actually *seen* the person perform. But if we've done a thorough job of executing our *behavioural* strategy for the interview, then we should have come awfully close.

Our interviewing should have allowed us to reconstruct past performance – to *re-create* it right there in the interview – *almost* as vividly as if we had in fact been there on the scene to watch it unfold.

So we know the candidate. And we are able, automatically and almost without conscious effort, to project that person ahead into a brand new situation and actually visualise their performance.

Making the decision

Having done that – having projected the candidate ahead into the new job and 'watched' them in action – we're now in a position to ask ourselves a very important question. *Do we like what we see?*

Do we like what we see enough to hire the person? Or, do we like what we see better than what we saw when we 'watched' candidates B and C and D perform?

When we begin asking ourselves these types of questions, we're moving toward the making of an actual decision with regard to the candidate. A decision to hire, to reject, to put on hold, or – in some cases – to ask them to come in again for one last go-around.

And there's nothing mysterious or particularly complex about how such decisions are made. We've projected the candidate into the job for which they are being considered, and we've actually 'watched' them perform.

Deciding what we want to do now should come as easily and as naturally as deciding whether or not we enjoyed a

> We're not really *predicting* anything, as most people assume. We're simply *reacting* to something we've seen.

particular movie, or deciding whether or not – now that we've seen the first half of the concert – we want to stick around and see the second.

We're not really *predicting* anything, as most people assume. We're simply *reacting* to something we've seen. That's why the decision is – or should be, at least, if we've done a good job of interviewing – such an easy and straightforward one.

In many ways, in fact, it's a decision that almost makes itself. Our task is simply to let it emerge, acknowledge it, sign the bottom line, and put it into action.

Is it really that simple?

In most cases, yes, it is. It's a bit like deciding which house you want to buy. Or which of six suits that you've tried on. The data doesn't need to be fed into a computer. You don't need an elaborate ratings sheet. You don't need to 'quantify' the decision or try to make it seem more scientific than it is.

You just make the decision.

And why shouldn't a *hiring* decision be just as easy? Think back to something we talked about at the very outset of the programme, when we laid out our *Behavioural* strategy for the interview. Imagine yourself being able to go out and watch each of five final candidates actually perform their current jobs, for one whole day.

Watch how they plan their day in the morning, if they do. Watch how they organise their time and decide what to do. Watch them as they call on people, talk to people on the telephone, interact with their colleagues, or talk and relate to their managers.

How do they deal with problems?

Watch, too, how they handle group situations. How they deal with tough problems or obstacles that they encounter during the course of the day. How they react when something goes awry, a presentation falls flat, a customer keeps them waiting in the lobby for twenty minutes or ushers them out the door before they've had a chance to cover the key things they wanted to cover.

Watch, too, what results they get. How those results compare to those of their colleagues. What help they got achieving those results. What sort of situation they were dealing with at the time.

If you could do all this, knowing who to hire would be very easy and very straightforward. You probably wouldn't even have to think about it. *The choice would be obvious.*

Or even if you simply had to predict how someone you knew well would perform in a whole new context. Imagine them getting up in front of a group and conducting a half-day training programme. How would they do? How would they perform? How would they actually *behave,* and what sort of *results* would that behaviour produce? *Would you hire them for the job?*

Again, the task would be a relatively easy one, even though we're predicting performance in a job which that person has never done before. In a context which they have not worked in before.

The secret is ... we *have watched the person actually behave.* Projecting that behaviour into the future – into a new job and a new context – is something we do intuitively. Which candidate do we want to hire? The answer's obvious.

We have watched the person actually behave. That's the key thing. And, if we've done a good job of interviewing, that's precisely what we've done. *We have watched the person actually behave.*

Isn't it all just 'gut feel'?

You might be thinking at this stage ... *Isn't it all just 'gut feel'?* And the answer to that, by and large, is *yes.* Not *entirely* 'gut feel' but there's no denying that essentially intuitive mental processes do have a role to play here. And there's nothing wrong with this.

'Gut feel' is something that the really good interviewers and decision-makers rely an awful lot on. Everybody knows that. Yet few people are able to explain what that mysterious substance is. Or how it works. Or how to go about acquiring it.

It is assumed that 'gut feel' is something elusive and ethereal, rather mysterious in its workings, almost magical in its power. Something, certainly, that can't very well be taught or learned or packaged for public consumption. Something you either have or don't have.

At this point, however, we should feel comfortable taking the opposite approach – and arguing that you *can* learn 'gut feel'. Arguing that 'gut feel' is nothing more than the systematic application of a definable interviewing strategy and a very tangible and teachable set of interviewing techniques. The same strategy and techniques, in fact, that we have been describing in this book.

The hallmark of the effective interviewer is the ability to go beyond the simple 'facts' of a person's background and gain insight into – or get a 'feel' for – the person themself. And then to go one step further and draw meaningful inferences about how well the person will perform in the job for which they are a candidate.

And the really good interviewers – you'll just have to take this on trust – use the process and the strategy and the techniques that we've been discussing right here in this book.

They may not describe the process in those terms. And they may not be able to elucidate the exact 'techniques' that they're using to implement the process. But what we have been describing here is basically what the truly skilful interviewers do. And it works.

Trust your instincts

Trust your instincts. That's something that you have to be prepared to do at this stage. And you can do it in *confidence* if you have really and truly taken a *behavioural* approach to the whole interviewing process.

Trusting their instincts is something that all good interviewers do when the time comes to *act* upon what they have learned about a candidate and make a final decision. And they can do it in confidence because of how they interview in the first place.

In the interview, they probe for specific behaviour, until they can almost 'see' the past unfolding before their eyes. And

> They can trust their instincts because of how they interview in the first place.

they search for patterns in that behaviour that will tell them what sort of person they are dealing with. And then they project that person ahead into the future and – again, in their mind's eye – 'watch' that person perform in the new job and under the new set of circumstances. And then they simply ask themselves how they feel about what they're watching.

So, if your instincts are telling you that yes, indeed, Susan is the person you want to hire...then you should be prepared to *trust* those instincts and move on them.

You should be excited

One last thing. You should feel *excited* about the idea of getting Susan on board and turning her loose. If you're not excited about it, then something's wrong. You *should* be excited. This is a big event. And there's great things to come. Susan's going to be an outstanding performer, and that's going to make our customers very happy and it's going to help us develop the business. And it's going to help *you* enhance your reputation as an outstanding *manager* who has this wonderful knack for picking winners.

So – quite seriously – you should feel a sense of *excitement.* You should feel enthused about Susan and about the prospect

> You should feel *excited* about the idea of getting Susan on board and turning her loose. If you're not excited about it, then something's wrong.

of her joining the team. If you're lukewarm, if you have doubts about what you're doing, if you're feeling something other than excited and enthused, then maybe you should stop and think about it. Because it's a sure sign that, in your own mind, you're either not totally convinced that Susan is going to be an outstanding performer or, what's worse, you *know* she's not going to be an outstanding performer – she'll be *good,* but not one of the top people in the company – and you're prepared to settle for that.

In neither case should you move ahead. Life is too short to be hiring someone about whom you are not enthused and excited.

Summary

In this chapter we have covered the very important stage of the interview process where you have to decide whether or not to hire one of the candidates.

◆ If what you did in the earlier stages of the interview process was carried out properly then this should be the easiest step of all.

◆ This is where you have to visualise how the candidate will perform *in that job*. We project their past behavioural patterns into the future.

I can just see it now

◆ You need to be able to 'see' the person's behaviour and hear the person's voice actually doing that job.

◆ You should know the candidate sufficiently from the earlier part of the interview to be able to do this.

Making the decision

◆ Do we like what we see enough to hire this person?

◆ Or do we just prefer this person to the others we've interviewed?

◆ It's just like deciding whether to stick around for the second half of a concert. We've seen the first half so we should know whether we want to watch the rest.

Is it really that simple?

◆ Yes.

◆ Have confidence in what you've done earlier in the interview.

Isn't it all just 'gut feel'?

◆ By and large it is because good interviewers rely on this as an extra, intuitive, skill.

◆ But gut feel is something that is enhanced with experience and you gain that experience by using a systematic approach to interviewing.

Trust your instincts

◆ This becomes much easier if you take a behavioural approach to the whole interview process.

◆ You will have seen the candidate's past unfolding before your eyes thus enabling you to project that person into the future.

You should be excited

◆ If you're not excited there's something wrong because this should be a big event. You're hiring someone who will help take the company forward and who should reflect well on you as a manager.

◆ If you have doubts about the candidate don't go any further. You have to be convinced that this candidate is a Winner.

We've got Susan on board. Our job now is to help her become a truly outstanding performer.

Final Thoughts

L et's close our programme with some final thoughts about the whole interview and selection process.

Nobody's perfect

Here's *one* important thing. *Nobody's perfect.*

No matter how much Susan impressed you, no matter how excited and enthused you are about getting her on board, she's not going to come in and *automatically* be an outstanding performer. It has to be *managed.*

And that's simply because nobody's perfect. There is always *something* that we have to keep an eye on or do something about if we want our best candidate to end up being our best *performer.*

In the case of Susan, it might be that she's not quite as aggressive as you'd like her to be in handling sales calls. She gets high marks on every other facet of the sales call, but she doesn't quite move things along as smartly and as proactively as most of our top people do. And it might make the difference between her being a *good* performer and a *top* performer.

◆ *What are you going to do about it?*
◆ *What's your plan?*
◆ *When does the plan go into action?*

Tough questions. But they have to be tackled, and tackling them is very much a part of the total selection process. Part of bringing a person on board is putting together a *development* plan, and a *management* plan, which will ensure that they end up being as successful as they deserve to be.

Scratch out a *development plan.* Let's call it by what it is – a *management plan.* The person's success is your responsibility. And their *becoming* successful is something that happens most directly through how the two of you *interact.* If Susan needs to become a bit more proactive in the sales call, you tell her that and describe the sort of behaviour you've seen that has led you to raise this issue. Compare that with the sort of behaviour that might produce a better result during the next sales call...

> The person's success is your responsibility.

What should we do now?

Behavioural managing. Not unlike *behavioural interviewing.* No one else can do this for you. And Susan won't end up being an outstanding performer unless you do it.

Not just Susan, but *everyone* you bring on board. There will always be something that has to be watched for and worked on. For example:

- Jim tends to be a bit of a worrier. He gets down in the dumps when results are slow in coming, or if things don't pan out the way he had hoped they would. You'll need to keep your eyes open for this sort of thing, and be prepared to sit down and give him a bit of a pep talk when it happens. You might, too, have to help him *lower his sights* a bit. He's expecting too much. He's being too harsh on himself.

- Paul's management style has a distinct 'edge' to it. Once or twice during the hiring process, we saw hints of impatience showing through. Not the sort of person who suffers fools gladly, we thought. And that's the way a manager *ought* to be. But now, three months into his new assignment, there's a bit of grumbling amongst his staff. He's pushing them pretty hard, and not always in as *positive* a way as might be ideal.

- Maureen's having difficulty dealing with the pressures being thrown at her by some of the people on the sales team. They waltz into the office like they owned the place – not all of them, but certainly a few of them – and they seem to expect everyone to drop what they're doing and attend to their needs. This memo has to be typed, that order has to be expedited, this package has to be delivered – Maureen's just going to have to learn to say 'no'.

♦ Jack's business judgement has come under scrutiny by some of his colleagues on the board. His decision to go ahead with the Manchester opening, in particular, is being questioned. We're beginning to realise that Jack's aggressive, full-speed-ahead approach – one of the main reasons he's a director to begin with – isn't always going to be an asset in a marketplace that's getting more and more complicated every day.

These are just a few examples of what we are getting at here. *Nobody's perfect*. There isn't a candidate in the *world* who can come in and be a star performer without learning something, or changing something, or doing something a bit differently from the way they've done it in the past. And it won't happen unless you exercise your managerial responsibilities and make *sure* that it happens. Not by signing the person up for the training course that's coming up a few weeks from now... but by *talking* to them. By being a coach. A catalyst. A facilitator.

Proactive recruiting

A final thought.

One of the biggest obstacles to good hiring is the *time* factor. If we're scrambling to fill a territory that's been vacant for two months, or if we're hurrying to get someone on board in time for the training programme that starts in January, then it's tough to do a really good job of hiring. And it's difficult to be objective when we sit down and ask ourselves whether we've got the best possible person for the job.

The best way to get around this obstacle is to avoid it altogether – by having a supply of good candidates available when we need them. Recruitment agencies will claim that this is *their* role, to ensure that such a supply is always available. But few of them deliver. They *hound* us incessantly when we *don't* need someone, and then have trouble delivering the goods when we're in a pinch and need to get someone on board in a hurry.

So they don't solve the problem. In fact, they make it worse.

Be your own recruitment agency

They make it worse because they lure us into forgetting that it is *we* – the managers – who should be carrying the ball. It is we who should be operating as our own recruitment agencies. We must talk to good people *all the time*, keeping track of where they are, letting them know when we think a job might be opening up. Make sure they know that we're interested in them even if we can't move ahead and explore things at this particular time.

When someone writes to you out of the blue, expressing an interest in joining the firm, *do* something about it. If the person looks good, give them marks for taking the initiative and find a half-hour to sit down and talk to them.

If you've heard some really good things about someone who's with the competition, and you have some reason to think that they might not be entirely happy in their current position, *talk* to them. Schedule a lunch or a breakfast meeting. Find out how they feel about things, what they might be after, when they might be prepared to think about a move.

This is the kind of thing that most of us recognise as making a lot of sense but don't really get around to doing. There are just too many other things on our plate. But remember what we said a little while back. We were talking about what *Winners* do. And we said that *Winners* don't just prioritise what's on their schedule. They *schedule their priorities*.

Ferreting out the best people in the industry. Getting in touch with them and keeping tabs on what they are doing. Letting them know that you'd like to sit down and talk when the time is right – this *has* to be one of your most important priorities.

Do it.

Summary

In this chapter we have offered some final thoughts on what to do after you've hired a winner.

- ◆ Remember that nobody's perfect. A candidate doesn't become a winner the minute they start with your company. Their development into a top performer has to be managed by you.

- ◆ Draw up a management plan for the person that identifies their strengths or shortcomings.

- ◆ Work with them on their strengths so that there is always something successful to report and realistic targets to meet.

- ◆ Work with them on their shortcomings so that they can see progress on a regular basis and so that their confidence isn't undermined.

- ◆ Be supportive.

One last thought

- ◆ Successful recruitment is a non-stop process. Always be ready for the unexpected vacancy if possible. Don't rely on recruitment agencies to do your work for you.

- ◆ They can't hope to respond to your urgent requests for potential winners. You must keep track of the type of people you wish to recruit and have them available when you need them.

Further Reading

How to Get Results from Interviewing, James Menzies Black, (New York: McGraw-Hill, 1970).

Taking Appraisals & Interviews, Jean Civil (London: Ward Lock, 1997).

Interviewing for Managers, John Drake (New York: American Management Association, 1972).

Conducting Effective Interviews, John Fletcher (London: Kogan Page, 1995).

The Right Man for the Right Job, Philip Marvin (Homewood, Illinois: Dow Irwin-Jones, 1973).

Readymade Interview Questions, Malcolm Peel (London: Kogan Page, 1988).

Recruitment & Selection, Philip Plumbley (London: Institute of Personnel Management, 1988).

Successful Interviewing in a Week, Mo Shapiro (Corby: The Institute of Management, 1993).

Hiring the Best, Martin J. Yate (London: Grafton Books, 1987).

Index